Part-Time Writer

Part-Time Writer

Marjorie Quarton

THE LILLIPUT PRESS
DUBLIN

First published 2010 by
THE LILLIPUT PRESS
62–63 Sitric Road, Arbour Hill
Dublin 7, Ireland
www.lilliputpress.ie

Copyright © Marjorie Quarton, 2010

ISBN 978 1 84351 166 3

1 3 5 7 9 10 8 6 4 2

All rights reserved. No part of this publication may
be reproduced in any form or by any means
without the prior permission of the publisher.

A CIP record for this title is available
from The British Library.

Set in 11.5 pt on 17.5 pt Caslon by Marsha Swan
Printed in Ireland by ColourBooks of Dublin

Contents

Foreword ix

Introduction xi

PART ONE: FICTION

1. Starting   5
2. Preparations   18
3. Stories and Courses   33
4. Characterization   43
5. Birth of a Book   52
6. Dialogue   60
7. Usage and Abusage   70
8. Narrative and Construction   91
9. What Readers Want and What You Can Give Them   101
10. Starting to Write a Novel   117
11. Getting down to Business   130
12. Going it Alone   143

PART TWO: NON-FICTION

13. The Same but Different   159
14. Memoir and Biography   176
15. How-to and How-not-to   188

Times are bad. Children no longer obey their parents and everyone is writing a book.
Cicero c. *43 BC*

Foreword

I can't claim to be writing this foreword in an impartial frame of mind. I once had the good fortune to be Marjorie Quarton's publisher so I came to know her, and to know her is to admire and like her, so I expected in advance to admire *Part-Time Writer*. I am, however, speaking the plain truth when I say that now, having read it, I admire it even more. I can't imagine a more sensible and helpful guide for the would-be writer, part-time or not.

Marjorie has turned her hand to many things, all of which she has done well. She has bought and sold horses, bred and trained sheepdogs, farmed sheep, been an antique dealer, run a charity – and in addition to all this has herself been a successful part-time writer who has helped other part-time writers towards success by running classes and by undertaking the editing of their work. It is from those last two parts of her career that she draws the wisdom and common sense that make this book so valuable.

It also reminds me of why I came to like Marjorie so much. There is no nonsense about it, and much wit and warmth, and it is also often very funny – see the section on sex and violence in chapter 9. In fact, that chapter is a good example of the book's unusual quality as a whole. The touch is light, but what is being said is profoundly *true*. Although Marjorie is often downright hard-headed about the practicalities of writing, she never takes the art less than seriously: she thinks it silly to write and then fail to do the best you can to present what you have written to readers, but at the same time she never doubts that writing is worth doing well for writing's sake. Her book will not only help people sell their work, it will also make them better writers. I think it will have a long and useful life.

Diana Athill

Introduction

I became a writer by accident. I slunk into writing by the back door. It would never have been possible for me to become a full-time author or journalist, because I am not and never was one of those who command six-figure advances and royalty cheques. Even if I were, I believe I would tire of authorship as a profession. The thought of sitting at a desk for a fixed number of hours every day fills me with a mixture of horror and boredom.

It is a fine thing to be able to describe yourself honestly as a writer, to know that you are one of a minority, in a profession generally admired and often envied. There is a thrill in seeing your name in print for the first time. (I don't count wild promises from *Reader's Digest* and the like: 'You are a winner Mrs Quarton!!!') I hope to show that you can achieve these things while being a part-time writer, practising an enjoyable

INTRODUCTION

hobby and collecting an equally enjoyable second income.

I come from a literary background and my mother urged me to 'write a book' when I was too young to have anything to write about. She mentioned Ernest Thomson Seton, the naturalist and writer, and his daughter, novelist Anya Seton. They were my relatives, as were Henry Seton Merriman, a fashionable author in the early 1900s, and Edith Somerville, a cousin. 'Of *course* you could write a book,' said my mother, aunts and cousins. My aunt, Evelyn Brodhurst Hill, wrote two successful books about Kenya and many articles for *The Spectator* in days when women who wrote political articles were scarce and treated with some suspicion. She used the painful nom de plume 'Eve Bache'.

I wasn't encouraged; I was alarmed. I felt I couldn't possibly measure up to my family's expectations. But still, I suppose a seed had been sown. I was over fifty when it finally germinated and I began, almost stealthily, to write.

I admit I was mainly motivated by money. In the 1970s, farming had improved, but drystock farming in Ireland was never a road to wealth. More importantly, two of our best sources of cash had dried up. Owing to the war in Northern Ireland, the British police forces were buying their remounts elsewhere and, even worse for us, the Swiss Cavalry had taken to motorbikes. Until then, our horse population had fluctuated between six and thirty and looking after them had been a full-time occupation on its own. We also had a kennel of working dogs and quantities of cattle and sheep. Write a book? When? How?

INTRODUCTION

I had already offered an article about working dogs to *Irish Farmers Journal* and had in exchange been offered £25 a week for a series of six. £150 would have bought a decent bullock. I was amazed. But I knew that specialized subject well, and the average farmer did not. So the work prospered and I did another series at £40.

What else did I know about? Horse fairs. I turned to *The Irish Field* and had a winter column with them for eight years. Later, I wrote books about working dogs and horse fairs, made money and learned that the pitfalls that face the specialist animal writer are deep and hard to climb out of. I had, however, taken the initial plunge, was known and accepted as a writer, and could risk asserting myself.

The first part of this book concerns fiction and I was never crazy enough to imagine that I could dash off a novel and expect anyone to publish it. But I used to take the magazine *Working Sheepdog News*, and send the occasional report. The editor asked readers to supply ideas for something to boost readership and wrote to me among others. The magazine was excellent of its kind, though in most families only the enthusiast was likely to read its worthy and solemn pages. I contributed a bit of nonsense called 'Sheep at the Sheepdog Trial', and it was so well received that I continued, encouraged by delighted phone calls and letters from people wanting 'More about Irish sheep'.

They got it. I wrote and wrote and found my little stories turning into a little book. I'll go back to those heady days later on. Heady, even though the magazine didn't pay me until

INTRODUCTION

years later. Once I had started to write fiction, ideas crowded my mind and I went about my work in a trance. Sometimes I asked myself why I had suddenly developed an urge to write; why I had imaginary people crowding my brain, waiting to have their stories put down on paper, why their doings were suddenly of importance, so that I felt obliged to write them down. They wouldn't leave me alone.

Many years later I gave a talk entitled, 'Should I Write a Novel? If so, how do I start?' Well, should you? If it clamours in your brain, demanding that you do something about it, then yes, you should.

For the past twenty-five years, I have been a part-time writer, combining it first with farming, horse dealing and dog breeding, later with a full-time PR job with a charity. I have never felt the urge to be a full-time writer, because I would feel pressure to achieve and nervousness about earning a living from it. I prefer to do what I can in my own time.

There's nothing wrong with working full-time as journalist or author. My warning is not to give up the day job until you are sure you won't regret it. When you have enough work on hand to give it all your time and attention and make a decent living as well, you can consider whether this is what you want or not.

When you give up work and start writing to a schedule, so many hours a day, will you still find fresh ideas? A life measured by deadlines is okay if you like your time to be ordered. If not, you might find the necessity of finishing a book, and starting another in order to keep a contract, mind-numbing.

INTRODUCTION

Writing should be a portable profession. Do you really want to turn your home into an office? Maybe you do, but working from home can be lonely and it's hard to discipline yourself when those fascinating ideas have dried up. Given that you can't just go away, shut the door and take a holiday, you might easily find that your new career was not a good idea. Not if you need to earn a living.

This book is a guide, based on courses and workshops I have held over a number of years. I know they work, because of the success rate of those that attended them. Students have been published for the first time, have continued to be successful and have won literary prizes. Latterly I have edited more than thirty books, mostly by first-timers and have had the pleasure of seeing several of them published. I think this has taught me almost as much as the writers I edit.

As a working model in the fiction section, I have chosen one of my novels, *No Harp Like My Own*. I use it to describe the gestation and birth of a middle-of-the road work of fiction. It has been quietly successful for more than twenty years, so I feel it is suitable, especially as it was a second novel, expected by my publishers to do as well as my first, which, eventually, it did. It's the only one of my novels to be contemporary (well, it was in 1988) and not a researched period work.

I don't believe in teaching something that I don't feel capable of doing myself. That is why this book is called *Part-Time Writer*.

Part-Time Writer

PART ONE

Fiction

1. Starting

Are you a teenager? A busy twenty-something? A harassed housewife – or husband? A pensioner with time to spare? Perhaps you are wondering how you could fit in a serious attempt at writing. Don't despair. There are many ways of combining a writing career with regular paid work.

I don't mean to aim at college students in this section, because the best way of getting published for them is by way of a degree in journalism. Young people with a talent for writing fiction generally feel the need to use it. There is little similarity between a young person's writing and that of an adult who has picked up thousands of ideas and tricks of writing along the way. The work of someone under twenty-five, however, has a freshness that doesn't last.

There is far more support for young aspiring authors today than there was a decade back, but the chances of getting fiction published are slighter than ever. To offset this, there are opportunities for publishing online, and most of the vanity publishers have disappeared or turned respectable. They have re-emerged among the print-on-demand and subsidy houses.

It is possible to study 'Creative Writing' at some universities and accepted summer schools, where much depends on the tutor. Great to be tutored by the likes of David Rice, Frank McCourt or Roddy Doyle, but qualifications for teaching writing as a career are founded on academic success as much as the ability to pass it on. As in almost every branch of tuition, naturally talented teachers often inspire their students to open up and forget their inhibitions, while others, as well, or better qualified, overawe their pupils, making them self-conscious about showing their work to the great man or woman. Or they may play safe by writing exactly as instructed, nervously keeping their gifts out of sight.

All these options are aimed at full-time employment and a career in writing. I mention them so as to give a general idea of what is on offer. Now I want to consider less permanent options.

The other thing to emphasize is the fact that it's seldom too late to start. There is so much support for young people who want to write, so little for the elderly. I was once interviewed for the post of Writer in Residence in Portlaoise. I didn't get the job and I was told that the main reason was that I was reluctant to work with the prison inmates, suggesting instead writing sessions for retired people and those living in nursing homes.

1. STARTING

In most retirement homes, elderly people would love to be visited by authors and perhaps take classes in short-story writing. I was born in 1930 and have edited for people of my own age group, who have been delighted with their new skill. Then there are the Active Retirement groups. For anyone retired and bored, writing could be something to try out for fun, then taken up seriously if the person developed a latent talent.

The basics

Bernard Shaw, on one of the rare occasions when he was forced to address students, asked what they thought was most essential to become a writer. A brave soul at the back suggested a pencil. Shaw's reply is not on record. Probably it was scathing. He once stated grandly, 'I was born a writer'.

The student had a point. A biro will do to start with, or a BlackBerry if you are so inclined. To begin, you need the simplest essentials, just enough to jot down ideas as they occur to you.

Too often, hopeful writers are over-faced by a mass of information, when what they need to know is the answer to the simplest questions. Is it in me to be a good writer? Have I got what it takes? Am I wasting my time?

The answers are as simple as the questions, but note that I said a *good* writer.

You need talent, imagination, an inquiring mind, above-average powers of observation, a will to succeed, and confidence.

PART ONE: FICTION

Talent

Talent may be anything from a timid aptitude to a towering God-given gift. If you had none at all, you would be unlikely to want to study the art of writing. You might like to learn about the craft of writing, which is different, or even the trade, but without talent, you would never be any better than average.

All talents have this in common: like neglected houseplants, without nourishment, they wither and die. You have a talent for self-expression that you feel might be developed? I have news for you – the simplest way to develop talent is to use it. Use it or lose it. If you don't use the gifts you were born with, they will atrophy and waste away. This is a particularly harmful wastage and it happens all the time.

Teaching an untalented person to write is like teaching a tone-deaf student to play the piano. It's possible, but the resulting performance has no soul, however correct it may be. I have spent many days and weeks trying to train untalented horses to jump and untalented dogs to round up sheep. Sometimes the results were passable, but I had spent too much time and, once I stopped actively training the animals, they stopped improving and lost interest.

Before you accuse me of likening you to an untalented sheepdog, look back. You must have some aptitude or you wouldn't be bothering to read this, so let's assume you have it and intend to use it. If you want to train your body for athletics or muscle tone, you exercise it regularly in whatever way is appropriate. The more you carry out these exercises, the easier they become, until they are part of your life. If for any reason you stop training, your muscles will go flabby after a while. If you don't use your talent, the neglected part of your mind will grow flabby and you won't be able to use it to advantage. How could anybody construct a plot or create a convincing character with a flabby brain? You must practise.

Imagination

Imagination is the thing that brings your gifts to life. Like talent, you were born with it. Like talent, it can be smothered and die of neglect. Almost all children have vivid imaginations. I think this is part of our Stone-Age history. A caveman's automatic reflexes were born of imagination. Today, if you are startled, your reflexes make you stand still, so that the sabre-toothed tiger may not notice you. The blood drains from your face, so that it can be concentrated in heart and muscles, enabling you to fight harder or run faster. Your sweating palms and soles cling to the bark, as your terror propels you up the nearest tree, with, if you are male, your genitals neatly drawn up into your body, out of reach of teeth and claws.

Children are simpler than adults. They may have real awareness of the wild animal sharpening its claws. In nightmares, they see things they have never seen when awake and, given the chance, they tell highly coloured stories. My daughter, aged about eight, was given a subject for an essay, 'What I did in the holidays'. She thought the reality far too tame and wrote about an imaginary safari, climbing trees to escape from wild beasts. She ended up by frightening herself and I don't think her teacher was impressed. Schoolwork is less inhibited today, but children who make up stories are still scolded for lying, which is another thing altogether.

Probably it is this early repression that makes many adults afraid to imagine. Or perhaps it's a lack of confidence and the fear of being laughed at – I don't know. When judging short-story competitions, I have read entries by adult beginners that didn't 'live on the page', because their writers had straight-jacketed their imaginations.

Some writers are sustained by the power of their imagination. They gallop from one unlikely scene to another and their readers follow, convinced. Luckily for those writers, fantasy, science fiction and grown-up fairy tales have made a comeback. They can thank Tolkien, Pratchett and Stephen King. Consider the Booker-winning *Life of Pi*. I don't know how the author got his book accepted, but I'll bet it wasn't on the strength of a synopsis. But, as one impossible scene follows another, the reader is caught up in the narrative. Yes, it's crazy, but what happens next? You need to know. This is the power of the writer's imagination carrying readers along with him.

Training your imagination is an essential part of using your talent. Observe people at work, on trains or buses, sitting on park benches. Using only what you can see and hear, build likely personalities for them and invent stories about them. There are no limits at all to what you can imagine. That big woman is a man in drag (look at her hands!). That little man scuttling by with a briefcase is an axe murderer when the moon is full. I do this in waiting rooms and airports as an antidote to boredom. I have sometimes found usable material like this – and occasionally become so absorbed in my fantasies that I've failed to hear my name being called.

An enquiring mind

This is a useful asset, often overlooked. If you weren't born with one, try to acquire it. Interest in other people and a willingness to learn are vital for a journalist, but make the fiction-writer's task much easier too. These qualities keep your mind and outlook young and your writing fresh.

You feed your inquiring mind by finding out the answers to the questions you ask yourself. If you can't discover what you want to know, ask. Or search the Internet. I shall have more to say about the Internet later on. If you don't use a computer, go the library, consult an encyclopaedia or specialist book on the subject. Read as widely as you can and use your critical faculties as you read. Try to keep your brain active always. I do word games and crosswords; other writers have other methods and there must be some form of brain-enhancement that you enjoy.

Powers of observation

These are essential to the journalist and writer of non-fiction, but useful for everybody. Powers of observation go hand in

PART ONE: FICTION

hand with memory, as it's no use observing if you forget what you've observed. You can train your memory and you should, but it's not a good idea to rely on it. Mine is vile and I carry a small spiral-bound notebook and use it. I say 'spiral-bound' because it's good to be able to tear out pages when you no longer need them.

I refrain from jotting down ideas when in company. People look at you oddly, and deplore your manners. Fix the material in your mind with one of the mind tricks of association that most of us use, and write them down later. When I'm researching, I use a reporter's mini-recorder. Talking to it as I google away is the quickest way to make notes. Pocket recorders are quite cheap and invaluable if your memory is bad. Tapes have almost disappeared, but I stay with my little recorder and its remaining mini-tapes, because I haven't found anything quite as cheap and simple to use. When it finally gives out, I'll get a grandson to explain the MP3 player to me.

The will, desire and need to succeed

Bracketed together, but all different. Desire and need are akin but dissimilar. They aren't the same as will or ambition. You can be a good writer and have no trace of ambition in your make-up. The will to succeed is a mixture of obstinacy and perseverance. Even if you are mild, quiet and retiring by nature, you can be determined to always do your best. You mustn't compromise. If your best isn't good enough for a particular publisher or editor, too bad, but you must be prepared

I. STARTING

to work hard in order to find out what you can do. The results may surprise you. Nobody walks into writing. Besides the determination, you need stamina, a love of words and a love of reading. The desire and need to succeed grow from this and will carry you along nicely once past the point where you are unsure if it's worth going on.

These are the emotions that keep you going when you are tired or disappointed. You shouldn't aim too high to start with, or you may be permanently discouraged. Tuition helps to keep you working when you might otherwise give up. This is partly reluctance to admit to your tutor that you are beaten. A good teacher knows when to encourage and when to criticize. To those godlike creatures who write perfect prose and claim that writing cannot be taught, I say ... well, I don't say anything. Who wants enemies?

The teaching of creative writing is really a misnomer. I can't teach anybody lacking in talent and imagination to 'create', only to copy and compose. I can teach people to develop the gifts they have and I can teach technique. Any tutor who claims to do more is suspect, but there are plenty who can and do teach the basics, with results to prove it.

Confidence

You don't need huge ambition, but you do need confidence in yourself and a positive mind. If you don't have it, try to develop it. Once you have successes, even small ones to your name, your confidence will grow naturally.

PART ONE: FICTION

When I started writing, I was a shy person. In fact, I still am shy. Many people who think they know me will fall about laughing when they read that sentence, but it's true. Shyness still surfaces if I find myself one of a crowd of people who know each other. I slip away and lurk near the door, wishing I were less tall. Now, public speaking no longer fills me with dread. In my early days, I turned down the chance of speaking on radio more than once. The first time I was interviewed on radio, I lay awake most of the night before, sweating with fear. Later, I turned down an appearance on the *Late Late Show* to my publisher's understandable fury. I might have gone through with it, had not some liar told me that Gay Byrne didn't like women, dogs or Protestants. When I eventually crept on stage in *Kenny Live* I was terrified. Only Pat's calm acceptance of my nervousness got me through the evening. He wrote a piece in *RTÉ News* about it afterwards, quoting my frightened comment, 'The dentist has a charming smile.'

If you lack confidence in the quality of your writing, I advise you not to show your work to your friends. Having it dismissed as nonsense or worse, boring, can dent your self-esteem seriously. Tell yourself that the critic may easily be wrong. Being too close to your critic is just as bad as being slated by a stranger in a book review.

Funnily enough, many people think they have a perfect right to criticize a writer's work, dismissing it in a few cutting phrases. These self-styled critics wouldn't dream of finding fault with your dress sense, your taste in men or women as applicable, or your baby's looks. This is a problem with some writers' groups, although I admit, many people swear by them. People judge one another's work and often, the most critical are the least fit to judge.

The first-time writer is a sensitive creature as a rule, quick to imagine a slight to his or her work. You must not react. If you expect praise and get, 'I expect I'll read it if I get time', it's hard to smile as you sign the copy.

Consider the probable feelings of Edward Gibbon, when he presented the second volume of *The Decline and Fall of the Roman Empire* to King George III, whose response was, 'Another damned thick square book, Mr Gibbon! Always scribble, scribble, scribble! Eh, Mr Gibbon?'

Somebody possessed of all the requirements mentioned, from talent to confidence, should be able to write for profit as well as pleasure, although I will concentrate on the pleasure aspect for the moment, because the pleasure of starting to write a novel, knowing that you may succeed, is intense.

Education

This extra heading occurred to me when being told for the hundredth time by well-informed, intelligent people, 'Oh, I could never write; I haven't the education.' Lack of education comes high on the list of popular excuses for not writing. Really, it's useful but not essential. My own education was patchy to say the least. I learned to read and write very young, did some lessons at home and didn't go to school until I was fourteen and a half. It was the middle of the school year and I had only just reached long division in arithmetic.

I was naturally good at English and liked the sound and shapes of words, as I still do. I don't think you need to be brilliant at English as a subject, although it helps. The feeling for language and words, which should be part of a writer's make up, is much more important than a degree in English. Maybe you wouldn't have got the degree without it, but not everybody has had the chance to study. The feeling for language can be cultivated, especially by reading. I have more to say about this in chapter 7.

Publishers' editors deal with serious grammatical errors. If bad grammar was enough to condemn a book, there would be no more tough thrillers. As long as you know what is correct, you needn't consider your grammar any more than you do when you talk. Most writers develop little ungrammatical tricks of writing. When they succeed in a big way, these are considered to be attractive hallmarks of an author's style. They may well be worth fighting for with publishers and editors, but be careful not to endanger a contract. Raymond Chandler wrote to his publisher, 'When I split an infinitive, Goddammit, it stays split …'

As for spelling, it isn't a handicap unless it's really appalling. Spellcheckers can't help if you spell a word with two meanings. Saying 'coarse' for 'course,' or 'paws' for 'pause', bewilders any spellchecker. If you spell so badly that you don't know the initial letter for neumonia – sorry, pneumonia – your dictionary won't help either.

I. STARTING

Spellcheckers are only as good as their compilers, so you can't always trust them. One of them, baffled by 'Jesus' came up with 'Jeans' as an alternative. A Dutch lady, Bea Zwagge, wanting to sign her work, was faced with the wiggly red underline. The spellchecker then offered the alternative, 'Beer Sewage'. 'Quarton' is corrected to 'Quarto'. You can't win.

2. Preparations

I hope you are not one of those people who can't use a computer, and are determined not to try. If you don't use one, you will handicap yourself unnecessarily, slow yourself up and generally miss out on much of the pleasure of writing. I know. I wrote three short books and two full-length novels by hand, then got them typed, with carbon copies. The process was slow, expensive and wasteful.

Not long ago, I found part of an early handwritten draft of one of those novels, all crossings out, addings in and angry notes to myself in the margin. They will be useful as it happens, because it is the book I mean to use for the purpose of explaining techniques. I often hear of famous writers, P.D. James is one, who still write every word of their best-sellers by hand. Well done, P.D., I admire you, but please, aspiring authors, don't feel that you must do the same.

2. PREPARATIONS

A few years back I was talking to a roomful of people about the desirability of using a computer. Most of them disagreed. Today, I'd be inclined to say the 'necessity'. Even then, there was much to be said for getting your work transferred to a computer after it was finished. The typewriter was becoming obsolete with editors and publishers. Now, everything has to be submitted in computer format.

'But computers are so expensive!'

'I couldn't possibly use one. I wouldn't even know how to turn it on ...'

'P.D. James always writes by hand ...'

'But things have changed,' I protested. 'Prices have come right down and machines can do much more, while they're easier to use. A laptop is ideal and unless you plan to put in dozens of photographs, or do presentations, a basic model will be fine.'

Still nobody was enthusiastic, although I know that a couple of them have taken my advice since. Some people are so rooted in suspicion that I have headed this chapter 'Preparations', to allay fears that I'm about to write on the finer points of computing.

One piece of advice that I can't emphasize enough is to get lessons in the use of a computer. You note that I didn't say 'take a computer course', this is quite a different thing. Those who set courses assume that the student will use their PC for everything, including keeping accounts, photography, graphics, website design and a load of other actions, most of them used only occasionally except by specialists.

PART ONE: FICTION

You could make a case for learning how to make databases and spreadsheets, but I assure you, they are things you can do without, at least for now. You won't need them for the purpose of writing. I've met dozens of people who have been put right off using a computer by the wealth of information that is crammed into a standard course.

Everything printed is in a computer somewhere. I don't know of any publisher or editor who accepts copy from a typewriter. Some accept e-mail attachments, some don't. CDs are an accepted way of sending manuscripts. If you are a beginner, who uses the computer to type only, you should still buy a modem to send and receive e-mail. Leave the Internet alone until you are happy and secure writing and editing your work.

I bought my first word processor when I had a fast-approaching deadline for a novel. The instruction book had been translated from the Japanese – it was a Japanese machine. Even when I was familiar with it, the booklet made no sense. I would have finished my book more quickly if I'd stuck to the typewriter I'd traded in. The word processor, which was quite complicated and had a short memory, cost £1000, which made a huge hole in my advance. A basic laptop today, portable but sophisticated, could cost €400 or less.

Two years later, I bought a computer, had two hours' tuition and plunged into the paperwork for an international sheepdog trial. I lost files, lost my head, my temper and many hours of sleep. Buy new equipment when you have plenty of time to spare.

2. PREPARATIONS

Not using a computer is expensive. If you want to publish – and who doesn't? – you will need to pay somebody to scan your typewritten files into a computer and save them to a CD, where you won't be able to access them yourself. For the floppy disks we relied on are supplanted. By the time this book appears, no doubt CDs will have gone the same way, in favour of flash cards.

As for the expense, you can still congratulate yourself on having chosen writing as a hobby, rather than photography or playing the harp.

Making photocopies of a 500-page manuscript, postage, return postage: these were a necessary nuisance and expense. You are still going to produce a manuscript in hard copy (printed MS), but now preliminary submissions can usually be e-mailed.

I'd find it hard to manage without my computer (and just about impossible to edit professionally) but I wrote my first book and dozens of articles by hand in large clear script, using narrow-feint note pads, A4 with margins to keep the copy tidy. They were accepted. I still type with two fingers, but I type fast. I was in my late fifties when I first used a typewriter, mid sixties when I graduated to word processor and almost seventy when I bought my first computer. I had no formal training, because I was using the machine so much. I had to pick it up as I went along. But I did pick it up – it's surprising what obstinacy and sheer bloody-mindedness can achieve.

When you get ambitious and want the very latest technology has to offer, it will be expensive. And you need

PART ONE: FICTION

patience and commitment to learn the use of all the gadgets. By the time you can honestly say you need these things, you are more likely to be able to afford them. My typewriter and computers were bought out of writing money paid for by my hand-written efforts. I never spend money on writing-related accessories unless I've earned it by writing or editing.

If you are experienced with a computer when you start writing, be careful. Knowing that you can alter or delete so simply can have a bad effect on your prose. You can often recognize the computer ace when you read a novel. It's full of padding and waffle. Waffle and padding are death to a short story and dangerous in a novel. The loss of 100 pages or more would improve some novels. So alongside the task of learning to write on a computer goes the hard lesson of brevity.

Buy a decent printer. It doesn't have to be a scanner, photocopier and fax machine as well, you can manage without those: just an honest-to-God printer. Get advice from somebody who uses one all the time. Remember some of them aren't as cheap as they look because they can be very hard on ink and cartridges are expensive. Printing a page makes it seem different somehow; it's easier to spot mistakes.

I use two printers, a Canon Inkjet and an HP Laser Jet. Lasers are still a bit unwieldy, suitable only for a location where they can remain permanently. The toners are hellish dear, although both this and the size of the machines will alter. The Canon is portable and the quality of the printing is much better. I use it mainly for graphics and photographs. The Laser is more suitable for long runs of print, such as a book.

2. PREPARATIONS

Once you have started, writing costs little besides time. You can begin when you are young, you can continue when you are old. Neither age nor poverty is an excuse for not writing. Disabled people have turned out excellent literature. You are offered enormous freedom of choice; you need only tackle what you feel you can do well. Better still, it gets easier. Subjects like mathematics get progressively more difficult, but the more you write, the more you will be capable of writing.

Since I started, some wonderful how-to books have appeared. I was a little bit miffed when somebody gave me a copy of *Computing for Seniors* and I found it condescending, but the *Dummies* and *Complete Idiots* books are fantastic.

You should consider buying some reference books. 'Google it,' they say, and we do, but the Internet doesn't really replace a good dictionary. My staples are these:

THE OXFORD CONCISE DICTIONARY

You don't need its big brother, it weighs a ton and is full of stuff nobody could need. Call me a Philistine. I've used both.

THE COLLINS THESAURUS

Is much easier to use than *Chambers* and a hundred times easier than *Roget's*, the best-known thesaurus, which lives splendidly on its reputation. *Collins* and the *American Webster's Collegiate Thesaurus* are arranged for easy access; *Chambers* is laid out like *Roget's* with cross-references.

PART ONE: FICTION

BREWER'S DICTIONARY OF PHRASE AND FABLE.
'Thesaurus' means treasure chest, a good description. I get sidetracked when I'm looking things up, but researching in *Brewer's* is even worse. It's not really a dictionary, but a fascinating source of derivations, old ways of speech, proverbs and legends and the nicest way of wasting time. I've also got the Irish edition.

THE OXFORD DICTIONARY OF QUOTATIONS
This book is really an indulgence. Again, it's easier to use than *Chambers* and more complete. It's the only source I know for the times when you want to quote and avoid misquoting and it can also supply a story or book title (just check the subject). Quotations and derivations must be accurate and you should verify what you've written. I used it to check the quote from George III to Mr Gibbon.

USAGE AND ABUSAGE
By Bernard Partridge. Based on the famous *Fowler's Usage*, I find it easy to use and often hugely entertaining.

Reference books are essential to me for editing. Sometimes I find words misused so that the sense is lost. I need to check in case I'm wrong myself.

I have collected these books over a number of years and they are old friends. At first they seemed too big and clumsy to be practical, but they are not. I never lend one and would rush to rescue them if there was a fire.

2. PREPARATIONS

I use two other dictionaries on occasion, both published by *Reader's Digest*. One is the *Wordpower* dictionary/thesaurus, an enormous book and the other is the *Reverse Dictionary*, mainly of use to Crossword solvers.

I use the Internet too of course, for research, but haven't found the dictionary part of it too helpful. As for Wikipedia … words fail me.

As a beginner, you will find it helpful to have everything you need to hand. Leaving the room to find a notebook, folder – or maybe the brandy bottle – breaks anyone's line of thought. Make sure you have elbow room on your desk or table, have a few biros that write freely, including coloured ones, spare folders, research material … everything you need.

I use lots of transparent plastic folders in different colours. They cost 50 cent each and are invaluable for collating your work and source material. Name each one in marker. If like me, you are not a tidy person, they will save hours of ferreting about among piles of papers, cursing and losing the thread of your narrative.

The things you need in order to write are so simple and basic that you might overlook them. A comfortable chair of the right height, which suits your back. Space on your desk. Paperclips. A stapler. A notebook. You do need a few difficult things as well and they can't be bought. They include a quiet, receptive mind and a relaxed body. The exception to this is the sort of person who needs a challenge, someone to bounce ideas off, or merely someone to snap at when things go badly.

As I am one of these people myself, I try hard to relax with little success.

Did you daydream as a child? I did and so did some writers I've talked to. I believe that daydreaming, a sort of unconscious way of writing a novel, can be deliberately harnessed to work for you. It works for me. Try to empty your mind when doing something boring like ironing. Then think about the story you are trying to write, but don't struggle to go on with it, just remember the last few lines you wrote and think of yourself sitting, writing them. I discovered by accident that if I did this, my mind processed what I'd been thinking and added to it quietly. The added bit would float to the surface when I sat down to write again. This last point is important, because I believe the act of sitting down and starting the computer triggered the memory.

Seriously, I think this process could be used, making your unconscious mind work for you in the background. We did it as children, left the half-finished daydream in our minds while we ate or slept, then returned to it and found it had been 'writing itself' while we were thinking about something else.

Taking the plunge ... or testing the water with one toe

Oddly enough, little seems to have been written for the writer who would love to produce a book or books, but doesn't want to take the risk of embarking on a new profession without a reasonable chance of success. I've looked through a dozen

2. PREPARATIONS

how-to books, many written by people with a nearly invisible track record, and all assumed that this poor beginner, who really didn't know how to start, was going to plunge into full-time writing.

This approach might suit an undiscovered genius toiling away in, say, the tax office. Be a full-time professional writer, if you have the nerve and the means, but not without experience, not without getting *something* published, plus commissions for enough work to keep you going for at least a year. Otherwise you would need an independent income, a saintly family and huge powers of endurance and concentration. And then you might never be published, unless by those firms that have to be paid more than the book will ever realize.

There is little in these how-to books to indicate that it is possible to ease yourself into your chosen brand of writing without bankrupting yourself and without having a degree. The budding genius will usually flower without help or advice from anybody, the person motivated by self-pity, vanity or spite would be wiser not to start. In between are thousands of people who need only some common-sense advice and some encouragment to use their talents, to be happier and better off.

There's disagreement about this point of view. Some fellow writers say, 'There's a book in everybody and that's where it should stay.' They forget the hundreds of thousands of published books that they wouldn't deign to read. These popular books make a living for writers and entertain readers. This is what they are for, isn't it? Some say not. This is where the divide in types of fiction comes in.

PART ONE: FICTION

The main types of fiction are, very broadly, literary, mainstream (or quality), popular and commercial. Genres such as crime, historical fiction and so on, cross all the divides. If you say that you can't have literary crime, you are wrong. Think of Oxford, always littered with corpses, according to several top crime writers. Seriously though, many crime writers would be up there with the award-winning literati if they wrote about almost anything else.

The main types overlap, but the literary end is written principally for the author's own pleasure; the pleasure of others and monetary gain being soft-pedalled.

A literary novel can have any form or none. It may be a long, closely written, 'difficult' book like *Finnegans Wake* or a slim wafer of a prose poem. It might have any kind of plot or none, or any kind of theme. The best literary novels can be enjoyed by anyone willing to give all their attention to what they read. I admit that this doesn't apply to all.

The other end of the scale includes all those entirely commercial, cheap, brightly jacketed books, which may be subdivided by their appeal to one sex or the other. These are the books that are read and reread until they fall apart and appear, ragged and filthy, in boxes at jumble sales. So you can't say they don't have a market; they have the biggest market of all.

The grey area in the middle includes what you might call quality or mainstream novels. I would have had no problem in separating popular from mainstream a decade ago, but they have grown closer together every year. Writers like Penny Vincenzi for example; those who feature smart, sassy

2. PREPARATIONS

heroines with relationship problems, are pushing the borders of the genre all the time.

In the charity bookshop that I oversee, I use the reviews quoted on the jackets to sort the genres. A tricky word, 'genre'; I've heard it pronounced to rhyme with Henry. *The Observer* and *Company* do not review the same books. Neither do *The Irish Times* and *Woman's Way*.

When just about to start my first novel, I went to a gathering in Dublin for the purpose of meeting an established writer of Literature (note capital L.) Shyly I approached him and murmured that I'd enjoyed his talk and was just starting to write myself.

'Really?' He raised his eyebrows. There was a pause. He then explained to me, quite kindly, that what he did was fiendishly difficult and so exclusive that a poor beginner was unlikely ever to be invited to join the club. 'Writers are born,' he said. 'There's no such thing as a period of learning.'

I wanted to ask him, 'Why then have you been telling us not only "how I did it", but "how you too can do it"? Were you never obscure, never inadequate?' I didn't, of course, but writing isn't a closed shop, available only to the exalted few, the possessors of a magical, exclusive gift. You can learn the technique. You can foster your latent gifts.

Talking to a celebrated writer may be what you need, but check them out first. The kind of literary snobs that treat their vocations as something up there with royalty and the priesthood are unlikely to help you. Such writers believe firmly that there is no room at the top.

PART ONE: FICTION

Evelyn Waugh was sacked from the *Daily Express* because, he was told, he couldn't write. He got his own back when he wrote *Scoop*, a savage satire on the newspaper world.

Everything I suggest or describe here is tried and tested. A rigid, inflexible writer can't really operate, because writing on the off chance of publication and large cheques is like playing roulette. Unwise unless you can spare what you spend.

As you plan how to fit authorship into your busy life, you are bound to need to compromise. In part, this means setting aside some time for yourself and, even more important, making the best use of it. Then, when you sit down to write for a couple of hours, you have something ready in your head, maybe some notes too. Later on, when your book is past the planning stage, you can try the daydreaming method, which may or may not work for you.

If you fail to come to your desk prepared and your mind is full of something else, demanding your attention, you can spend half your allotted time searching through old notes and telling yourself you are mad to try writing as a sideline. You must develop the habit of thinking ahead while doing things that require little thought. I still take this to extremes, being bad at doing two things at the same time. My poor husband was patient with me when I forgot to prepare meals. I used to go into a dream when I was writing a novel, once I was well into it. The actual writing took far less time than the dreaming. Once, as I constructed a conversation in my head, I drove straight past the turning to my home and a couple of miles down the road before I noticed. As I'd been living

2. PREPARATIONS

there for about sixty-five years, this was absent-mindedness gone mad.

I started out by buying all the writing materials I could afford, choosing a quiet time, sitting down at the kitchen table and awaiting inspiration. It was a painful, unprofitable period. I would sit looking at a writing pad for a whole afternoon, occasionally scribbling a note.

I gave it a rest for some time. Then my mother became an invalid and I couldn't leave her alone for very long. I had time on my hands for the first time in years. I knitted, and painted china to augment my income and thought about writing while I did it. An idea formed in my mind. An idea for a novel.

Back to the writing pad. Some days and 4000 words later, I decided that my idea wasn't as good as I thought it was. I returned to knitting, painting and thinking. I realized years later that the reason the idea didn't work out the first time was that I hadn't the faintest idea how to develop it. I tried to write a book putting people and incidents into it as I went along. The result was a long short story with a good basic idea, cardboard characters and a jumble of loose ends instead of a climax. Eventually, I used the best bits in a novel.

The writing of a middle-of-the-road novel requires more than technique to lift it out of the ordinary. It requires the writer's emotional involvement. My emotions at the time were a tangled mess, so I kept them out of my work. You can write a factual article or a readable interview and leave your emotions fermenting away elsewhere. But to write credible

PART ONE: FICTION

fiction, you need to use more than the surface of your mind.

When I began to think seriously about taking up writing as a part-time career, I returned to non-fiction, as more likely to pay, so I will return to that in the second part of this book.

When Pelham Books, a subsidiary of Penguin, gave me a £2000-advance for *All About the Working Border Collie*, I thought I was made for life, but it was the culmination of four years of articles in half a dozen newspapers and magazines. I could have made a living then as a full-time freelance journalist, but it wouldn't have suited my lifestyle.

3. Stories and Courses

Short stories

The embryo novelist, ready to start, needs to practise. And the best practice I know is to write short stories.

For the moment, forget the phantom publishers, the fame and acclaim. Write a story for the RTÉ Radio 1 Francis MacManus Short Story Competition. You may not win anything, but the shortlist is broadcast and writing for radio is amusing. There are dozens of short-story competitions and *Ireland's Own* has one that gets hundreds of entries. There are also competitions run by various writers' groups and literary festivals. Look on the Internet to find lists of competitions of all kinds.

I suggest entering competitions because for as long as I've been writing, short stories have been hard to place. Yet, many 'How to Write' books and most correspondence courses teach

PART ONE: FICTION

short-story writing and no other branch of fiction. Why is this? They come back like boomerangs from magazines and the beginner has little chance of placing even one.

When a popular novelist publishes a collection of them, it is named after the best, or sometimes the longest story in the collection. The information that you are *not* buying a new bestselling novel is sneaked in on the back flap.

I have only had about a dozen short stories published, aside from a children's storybook called *The Cow Watched the Battle*. Many that I wrote for practice have never been offered, but every one I wrote taught me something, helped me to encapsulate a subject and a set of characters without coming up with something that read like part of a novel. It is very hard to write a good short story, but I suggest that you try. I had the advantage of a good tutor.

My first appearance in print was an article in the *Irish Farmers Journal* and I had success there and later in *The Irish Field*. I was keen to write by then (I was fifty-three). My husband gave me a course with a writing school for my birthday.

The course arrived, a box of big imposing files and folders with embossed gold lettering, all promising success. The deal was that if you published during and as a result of taking the course, you didn't have to pay. I read the first assignment, on getting into print, with mounting dismay. My homework was a 300-word piece for the defunct paper *Titbits*. I wrote it, perhaps tongue in cheek, and encountered my course tutor John O'Toole. He was the senior tutor and without him I doubt if I'd have completed the course, which, like *Titbits*, is now defunct.

I struggled through two assignments, then I sent a letter to John O'Toole saying I wasn't getting what I needed – straight tuition in writing fiction. Boldly, I asked if I might just read the assignments, making notes, but instead of writing set pieces for various popular magazines, I would send him a short story with each one, for him to criticize and edit. John spoke to the directors, got his way and tutored me in fiction writing for the rest of the course.

By the time I'd finished it and gained a diploma, I'd sent in a dozen short stories and was working on a novel. John ran his own course in novel writing, probably the only one at the time, and I was struggling with *Corporal Jack*, my first full-length work. I took John's novel writing course and the book was a success, and still is around twenty-two years later. We didn't always agree and argued fiercely at times, but John's advice was sound and above all, he kept me writing. It was he who suggested the title 'No Harp Like My Own' for my second novel, and I continued to seek his advice right up to the time he retired.

One of his courses was chapter-by-chapter editing and tuition and, when failing sight obliged him to give up his work, John suggest I take up tutoring myself, using any part of his material that I might find useful. I still use an updated version of the course as part of my editing and tuition. Thank you, John.

The novel *No Harp Like My Own*, is my chosen model

PART ONE: FICTION

for explaining 'how I did it'. It doesn't pretend to be 'how you should do it, ,but I believe it will show how a glimpse of a viable character can build into something unexpected.

Part of *No Harp* first appeared as a short story. This had been written for practice, but the two editors I sent it to turned it down because the key character was an old person, and for half the story, a dead one. I will return to it later on.

Short stories provide you with a cache of usable material, characters, plots and incidents, that you can use in a novel. Many a big fat book sprang from a short story. As for material, it is all around you if you look for it and with practice that will be easy.

My first published story arose from a scary incident when I was alone at home late at night and heard a commotion out in the farmyard, where a hundred sheep should have been sleeping soundly in the barn. Thinking that a stray dog or a fox might have upset them, I went out with a torch in nightie, dressing gown and wellies.

When I went into the shed, my own dog rushed at the hay bales, stacked high above my head, barking angrily. There was a tremendous rattle of the tin roof, a slithering sound at the far side and a crash. I grabbed the dog and kept him with me. The Troubles were with us and certainly somebody had chosen the shed to sleep in. Whoever he was, he ran away and I went back to bed, shaking with cold and fright.

I later wrote a story called 'Stranger in the Night,' describing a young widow's encounter with somebody sleeping in her hayshed, who turned out to be on the run. The story told

3. STORIES AND COURSES

of the woman's helpless fear as she was obliged to let him into her house where he had a cup of tea and left, unexplained. My own experience allowed me to know exactly how Mary felt when the stranger slid down from the hay bales. Well, the story won an award in the *Ireland's Own* short-story competition and I sold stories and articles to *Ireland's Own* for some time afterwards.

Back to the blank sheet of paper, the empty screen. Try to think about something you might use before you settle down to work. It's easier to do this when you are doing chores around the place than when that screen seems to stare accusingly at you. 'Well, get on with it …' it seems to say.

It can be hard to think up a plot and characters, then sit down and write a story. I found a way of getting people to write fluently when I held a short-story course in Nenagh VEC. The students, who were of all ages, from teenagers to a man in his seventies, looked appalled when I suggested they should spend the next half hour writing. I'd given them a talk and hoped to find out what they'd made of it, being new to teaching. As they got out paper and Biros, looking unhappy for the most part, I happened to remember a letter I'd got from a friend who had witnessed a fire and couldn't wait to tell me about it. It occurred to me that this girl wrote better than she talked, very well in fact.

So I said to the class, 'There's been a bank raid in Nenagh. You were there. You are each going to write a letter and tell me about it. Maybe you were behind the counter, or a customer, or one of the raiders, I don't care. Maybe you drove the

PART ONE: FICTION

getaway car, or were a hostage. You want to write to me about it. So start, "Dear Marjorie," and carry on from there. I want an eyewitness account.'

Within a couple of minutes they were all writing and each completed an adequate piece of work within the half hour. Some were extremely good; none was bad. I noted with amusement that a quiet elderly woman chose to write as a raider and was the only one to carry a gun, while the lady with the most to say and the only man present to have had a story published, both chose to be terrified customers, lying face down on the floor, praying. Hardly an eyewitness account, but it gave another angle. The teenage boy who wrote as the driver of the getaway car, couldn't get away as he got caught up in a funeral procession and wrote it for laughs. He's been published too.

This worked so well that I have used the method myself when I wanted to write an action scene and found that inspiration had left me. I would imagine I had been there and was telling a friend about it in a letter. The method gets the imagination going nicely and I recommend it.

It's hard to discuss short-story writing because there are so many kinds, from the highbrow 'plotless' story to the simple narratives still favoured by some magazines.

I suggest that you think up an interesting character or two, a plot and a background and just start. I did that when writing a story every week for the course and having no idea what it was going to be about. Once you have thought out the plot, you should write an outline to keep you on track, as you need to keep a story tidily within a framework.

3. STORIES AND COURSES

Sometimes, you might hear of a true incident that would translate well into fiction. Here is a good example that I used myself. There was an elderly man, who walked on two sticks, who spent his days sitting on a kitchen chair in the street outside his home in a County Clare village. He was bad-tempered and people who stopped for a chat moved on again rapidly.

One summer, two of his nephews came from another part of the country for their holidays. The older lad, Paschal, was about seventeen and rode a motorbike, the other a couple of years younger. Their mother told them repeatedly not to bother Uncle Mick, but they didn't listen. They liked him, who knows why, and spent much of their time running errands for him and urging him to tell them stories of the days when he was young. Mick had been around during the Civil War and he told the boys things he'd never told anyone. They were thrilled, especially the younger lad, and the day before they were to leave, they announced that they were going to give him a treat.

'What's your favourite place in Ireland?'

'Lisdoonvarna,' said Mick, with a wistful look in his eye.

'We'll take you there on the bike.'

'You will not.' But they had very little trouble persuading him and on Sunday, they loaded him onto the bike and Paschal set off for Lisdoonvarna with him.

The man who told me the story was driving bullocks on the road and met Paschal with Mick on the pillion, 'going as fast as God would let them'.

Nobody was killed, but Mick finished up in Ennis Hospital. For some reason, the trip acted as a sort of catalyst. Not only did he leave money to the boys in his will, an unsuspected hoard, but he became quite chatty as he sat on the kitchen chair in the street, telling anyone who would listen how 'Mary's lad, Paschal, took me for a spin on the bike and, only for that hoor's cattle on the road, we'd have had a day out in Lisdoonvarna.'

It's a true story, but I couldn't possibly use it while Mick was around. Some years later, it morphed into 'Day Trip to Scarborough', a story about a bitter old retired governess living alone in Leeds without friends. Soured by a love affair gone wrong, nobody bothers with her until two teenage girls doing a school assignment on cheering up lonely people come to call. She sends them away, but something makes her call the older girl back … A friendship develops and, you've guessed it, after months of meetings, cups of tea and chats, the girl arranges a lovely surprise for Miss Mills. Her big brother will take her to Scarborough on his motorbike. And he does.

This story has been published and was read by Thora Hird on the BBC.

So much is common to both long and short fiction that writing a separate section for short fiction would mean repetition. As I deal with each section on novel writing, I will apply my findings to stories as well, pointing out likenesses and differences.

Short stories shouldn't be overpopulated. You need a couple of key characters (not necessarily a couple as in an item) around whom the storyline develops. There should be

3. STORIES AND COURSES

at least one person in opposition to them. The shorter the story, the less scope there is for developing a character and stories have been getting shorter and shorter. Magazines that used to feature at least three every week, plus a serial, now go in for snappy snippets instead. Stories have been replaced by fact (of a sort), mainly about 'celebs'.

Check out the magazines in your nearest newsagents, taking a quick look at the index of each. Then consider whether you would like to offer one of them something of your own. Try to write about 1500 words if you have characters and storyline assembled in your head. You need that amount to develop a plot. When I first wrote stories, 3000 words was a popular length and 2000 was 'radio length', allowing time for an introduction, a few bars of music and, on most stations, three minutes for a commercial.

Now, competitions often specify 600 words or even less. These 'short shorts' are harder to write well than a 'long long'. They need minimum adornment, everything pared to the bone and leading to a punch-line as quickly as possible. Structure must be simple but definite; characters have to be consistent. Someone said to me, 'Aim at the length of time it takes to drink a cup of tea.' You could have put away a five-course meal and still not have finished, when reading some of the old magazine stories.

Stories, like novels, can be broadly divided into 'commercial', 'quality' and 'literary'. As with novels, the purely literary variety is the least likely to make you rich, although you might have a literary festival named after you when you are dead. There are many subdivisions and the only way I know to discover what editors want is to read some of the stories they publish. The *Writers' & Artists' Yearbook* is sometimes lagging a little behind its subjects, but the section on magazines is valuable, including specialist publications, where you might find a slot for a story about an obscure subject that you feel able to discuss.

4. Characterization

Of all the qualities a writer needs, I rate most highly the ability to create a convincing character. Quite apart from the obvious need to put believable people in your stories, knowledge of characterization brings with it a deeper understanding of real people. The more you study, the more you discover. For me, the hardest part of writing, story or novel, is the preparation: the plotting and the shape of your work, the way it should develop. I have always put characters ahead of plot, so first I think up a character and let the storyline develop around this person.

My early writing was mostly about animals and farming. Occasionally I had to struggle with an interview, which I found incredibly hard. I reached the nadir on a windy March day in a muddy field, where I was required to interview a cold, cross man who had just watched his daughter win a ploughing competition. He was doing the interview because 'Mary's very shy altogether; she'd be in dread.' We shouted away into my little recorder, while the supposedly shy Mary yelled contributions over her dad's shoulder. He contradicted most of them. The result, when I played it back, was funny; my yelps of laughter made people look round as I sat in my wet clothes, warming up with tinned oxtail soup in the only hotel restaurant within thirty miles, but of course it had to be heavily edited. I was used to that, but this one was impossible. I couldn't turn it into something acceptable for the newspaper. Finally, I left it while I had some ham and tomatoes, then attacked it again, with more success.

My problem was lack of sympathy with Dad, who was more interested in getting his own name into the paper than Mary's, plus my lack of sympathy with Mary, who was determined that this should not happen if she could prevent it. Location didn't help; neither did the weather. When later I read the resulting article it was all right, but stiff and far from good.

When, in the course of learning how to write fiction, I began to build composite characters from actual people, I found I had to study those real people in a way I'd never done before. I learned to understand their motives much better, and interviewing came more easily after that.

It is possible to construct a person from a set of rules and put them in a story. Skilfully done, it almost works. You can describe every detail of their appearance, every gesture, every happening that has helped to make them what they are. You can build this person up like a model from a kit, using

4. CHARACTERIZATION

instructions on 'how to characterize', and you finish up with somebody who is almost a person.

Just as waxworks of the famous are so lifelike that you gasp – with delight or horror, according to your politics – but it isn't a politician. It isn't anybody. It's a clever copy of life.

Many published magazine stories and novels are peopled with waxworks, and they sell. This is because of the strength of the plot, the continuous action, or the humour of the situations. Such things make living, breathing characters unnecessary. Many branches of 'genre' fiction use stock characters, sketched in, given some trick of behaviour, some oddity of appearance to make them memorable. Many a heroine is nothing but a beautiful clothes horse; many a hero is no more than a macho robot. This sketching in is essential when characters are not properly thought out. If the book sells well and gets filmed, the movie may be much more memorable than the book, because it is inhabited by real people.

In a short story, your main character should be accurately but briefly described either right at the beginning or after the first important incident. Detailed descriptions don't work because we get fleeting impressions in real life: red hair, a Cork accent and earrings; a pot belly, tiny feet and pince-nez, for example. First impressions last, and are reliable. If you had been talking to a stranger for ten minutes and were afterwards asked for a description, you might be able to supply one if trained in observation. More likely you would remember a big mouth, untidy hair and, almost certainly, the person's voice. You remember the feature you watch as you speak – eyes or mouth, whichever is the more remarkable. The colour and style of clothing is quickly forgotten unless really outrageous; gestures and tones of voice have more power to impress.

Describe your key character in few words, but keep them vivid. Then, if the story is long, you can add to the description later on, preferably in small doses.

In older novels, writers have gone to considerable lengths to describe appearance without listing features and colouring. The 'show, don't tell' method of writing made things much easier. Here is Lesley in *No Harp Like My Own*, when Ben sees her for the first time: 'He noticed that she had a long nose and a short chin and you couldn't call her pretty ... she turned her head and he saw her broad forehead and that she had intelligent eyes and a gentle mouth ...' This description is longer than normal, for a reason, but it's still what was glimpsed in a couple of seconds.

Quality stories use more description of their characters' natures and thoughts than purely commercial ones. This is because quality writers can dredge up interesting turns of phrase and unhackneyed words. This takes practice, or a powerful natural ability.

Now for the difficult part – to make the waxwork live. For this, you must know the person's make-up before you start to write about an isolated episode or series of episodes in his life. Your readers don't have to be let in on this, but they will be able to believe in a character who is in an 'ongoing situation'. (Hateful expression, that. It's on my black list, but it can be useful.) The biggest mistake is to start your character's life

4. CHARACTERIZATION

on page one. More often than not, it starts at a crossroads in the key character's life.

I have got myself into fierce arguments over the years by insisting that character should come before plot in a novel. I like to think up a character, perhaps based on a real person or a conglomerate of two or three. I think about this person as much as possible, adding things and sometimes rejecting them. By degrees, the character becomes real to me. He or she begins to live. Once that happens, you are half-way to the plot and the other principals in your work. People make things happen. Things don't make people happen.

All of life is a chain of cause and effect. Everybody is motivated by something. The plot should seem to be the natural outcome of the natures and actions of the characters. They should act out the story within a plotted framework, developing from a point known to the author, maybe back in childhood. Characteristics such as greed, optimism and cruelty can often be traced right back to babyhood. The writer should know what makes people tick. The reader may or may not be let in on the secret at a later stage.

To develop this thought even further, I firmly believe that if your character is to live dramatically, so that every reader remembers him long after the story is read, you have to give him life. The only life available to you is your own; you must put something of yourself into this imaginary person. Good or bad, male or female, it makes no difference. That is the only true way to make the waxwork live. Ask yourself, 'If I were this person, how would I react to these happenings?

PART ONE: FICTION

How would I feel?' Then adjust your findings in line with the person's age, sex and position in life.

Feel for and with your characters, don't hold yourself aloof and merely comment. There's no need to be self-conscious, no need to bare your soul. Simply care about the people in your work – that will do.

When you need to 'get to know' a character, in order to convince, try what actors do and think your way into the skin of the person. It takes patience and time, but in my experience it pays off.

In a love story, I would hope to identify with the heroine, to feel with and for her, but it isn't vital as long as you believe in her. Belief in the people you have invented is necessary, as it helps you to know how they will react in any circumstance. 'Hero' and 'heroine' by the way, suggest Mills & Boon and the like. The alternative, 'protagonist' sounds stilted to me but must suffice. I vary it with 'key character'.

All the above is valid for a novel or a short story, but the shorter the story, the more compressed the character must be. Just as, later on, you will learn how to take the essentials of a conversation and discard the rest, so in a story you use the pared-down character, because there isn't room for anything more. In a story, you falsify life because there is only room to show certain facets of character – a few incidents in a lifetime. You use what is relevant and produce a complete, rounded work.

Does this sound like too much trouble? Wrong – it saves trouble. A properly thought-out character is easy to direct, a

4. CHARACTERIZATION

cardboard one is not. They sometimes have to be killed off to get them out of difficult situations. This is not good writing. A rounded, three-dimensional character can act surprisingly and still convince – a flat one doesn't alter. Nobody is without surprises.

We all draw on life; we must – but we can only describe somebody whose thought processes we can understand. We make composite characters, skipping the difficult bits. People are too elusive and shadowy to be copied anyway. We take what we need from them.

Don't make your key character perfect. A person with no faults will read like a pompous prig. Another thing: it's very hard to make a totally good person live. There's no place in literature for total goodness, or in life either.

Hard as it is to write about the wholly good, it's impossible to write about the utterly bad. Graham Greene set out deliberately to do this in his novel, *Brighton Rock*. He found his task next to impossible. The character, Pinkie, is too bad to be true. Greene was trying to describe what doesn't exist in nature and he almost succeeded but not quite.

Be careful when you describe a real villain. They don't usually appear to be villainous, while many scary bikers with raucous voices and tattoos all over them are likely to be loving partners and caring parents. Besides, the swaggering gunslinger has a sort of fatal attraction. Greedy, spiteful or cowardly people are more hateable. Bad women are known for being attractive (although not to other women). In modern fiction, baddies are often glamorized and often female. It's up to you. You may not need or want to write about extreme characters. Then don't. However, you must have contrast in your characters.

If you want your readers to like them they must not be feeble. Your protagonist might be home-loving, peaceable, shunning the limelight, but never feeble. Strength of purpose, integrity and often humour make a low-key person interesting in the same way that humane instincts can make a vicious character interesting.

What's in a name? Does the name of a character matter? Writers of romances think so. Barbara Cartland said that a heroine's name should always end with an 'a' and not be too long, while her heroes have one-syllable names ending in a consonant. Thus, Cecelia and Dirk, Amanda and Bob, Lavinia and Bill. You can see a kind of logic in this, given the author's style and themes.

I find it hard to shape a character that I haven't named. 'Use a working name,' say the manuals. No good. The person has to have his or her real name and, once I find it, the character takes on extra life and meaning. In *Renegade*, which is a true story, I was stuck with Henry and Anne, not names I would have chosen. However, the method worked in reverse as, once I'd got to know my characters, their names didn't matter.

If you write about a real villain, be careful in naming him. Give him a name so common that nobody is going to accuse you of libel. Plead ignorance if this character is called Paddy Murphy or Jim O'Donnell. If you called your villain Lionel Ramsbotham and there happened to be a law-abiding citizen of that name in the area, you would have some explaining to do. Again, you could think you were picking a name out of the air, but really it might have been lurking in your brain, having been heard and noted months before.

I would advise you to avoid the name of the moment as it will date and avoid anything too unlikely, unless you are being funny. You can use simple names, perennially popular, for your key characters, but you may find yourself drawn to something less likely. Agatha was fine for the seriously screwed-up old lady in *No Harp Like My Own* but not for the principal female character.

5. Birth of a Book

Really I should have called this chapter 'Conception of a book'. Birth is a long way ahead: a lot more than nine months.

The seeds of a short story came to me when I was skimming through a book of poetry and noticed the 'Scholar Gypsy' by Matthew Arnold. I had read the poem at school and it had the usual footnotes. The idea for the poem came from a sentence: 'To be completely single-minded is to be immortal.' As the poor ghost was eternally seeking the 'Divine Spark'.

Nobody, but nobody, was as single-minded as my paternal grandmother, Caroline Smithwick. I was afraid of her. My mother disliked and avoided her, my father claimed to admire and respect her, although they couldn't be in the same room for ten minutes without an argument. The irresistible force met the immovable obstacle and neither would give way. It was lucky that she didn't visit often. When she did,

5. BIRTH OF A BOOK

she instructed my mother to call her 'Mother': this was too much, and my mother stuck to 'Mrs Smithwick'.

If I misbehaved as a child, the worst threat my parents could think up was, 'If you aren't careful, you'll grow up exactly like your grandmother.' When she died, my father got letters from people he'd never heard of, saying what a lovely lady his mother was. So kind, so unselfish … Apparently she had helped a great many people in a lot of ways. She kept this from her family.

In her youth, she had been a woman about a hundred years ahead of her time. She was a red-hot republican and an advocate of free love and birth control; this when she was the wife of the Protestant rector of Monasterevin. She had love affairs and espoused unpopular causes with such panache that nobody could pretend not to notice. My grandfather died of cancer in his forties, by which time he was Chancellor of St Patrick's Cathedral in Dublin. Granzie, as her family called her, had found a new cause in the slums that surrounded the cathedral, where she did a great deal of good. There, she met Maud Gonne, who was a kindred spirit, although I believe they fought a lot. They distributed hot dinners together and Granzie went with Maud to the Mayo Evictions. Yeats, she dismissed as a 'silly little man'.

Later she became a militant suffragette and chained herself to the Trinity College railings. The police refused to send her to prison, to her fury.

Her character fascinated me when, as an adult, I began to consider writing. The family went into collective shock when

PART ONE: FICTION

I suggested a book about her, so I shut up. However, that seed lay dormant and was fertilized, so to speak, by the 'Scholar Gypsy'. For tenacity and single-mindedness, Granzie would have put a pitbull to shame.

My short story featured an old woman, whose iron determination to keep the family farm and to see that her son married a suitable person to help run it became an obsession. In the story she becomes bedridden and continues to run everyone and everything. Her son creeps past her door because, if she hears him, she calls out, 'Is that you, dear?' and is ready and waiting to manipulate son or daughter-in-law by means of emotional blackmail.

When she dies, the family takes a holiday, returning lightheartedly to their home a fortnight later, but when the son passes that door, he hears a quavering voice with undertones of steel, 'Is that you, dear?'

I knew I couldn't write a novel about an old woman, but I didn't intend to waste her either. I wondered what would happen if two people had the same genes, so that they were identical in their initial make up. I decided I'd give Agatha, as I'd decided to call her, a grandson who was her double. The daughter in the intervening generation would be a colourless woman, having been under Agatha's thumb, or heel, her entire life. The young man was modelled on someone I'd gone out with, years before, both in his appearance and his way of speaking. I named him Ben after a favourite dog, but I liked the name anyway.

I thought for ages about ways of handling these charac-

5. BIRTH OF A BOOK

ters. It was obvious that Agatha would take a violent dislike to anyone Ben brought home, so I sent him to Yorkshire, the only part of England that I know fairly well, Ben having walked out after a row with Agatha.

It bothered me that if I was going to make Ben into a likeable enough human being for readers to care about, I was going to have to deal with him in a convincing way. I'd thought about Agatha and given her a traumatic experience that had unbalanced her. It had also taken her away from her family and planted her on a moderate farm in County Kildare.

To carry the storyline through, Ben was going to have a traumatic experience too. But instead of throwing him off kilter, it would, in the long run, be the making of him. He was a difficult, moody young man, with some excellent character traits. He fell in love, as planned, with Lesley, and then I got into a writer's block, which would have defied a plumber to sort out. I kept doggedly writing, because my first novel was doing well and Collins wanted another.

The book dragged, the storyline refused to develop, I wrote and rewrote endlessly, until something clicked in my mind. Then the story came together so fast that I couldn't keep up with it and kept having to check what I'd written. This was the scrambled and blotched manuscript I mentioned earlier. I was too slow to type and think at the same time. The computer was in the future.

This is how an unexpected happening dislodged the block, fed me with material and set me on a roll that lasted until the end of the book.

PART ONE: FICTION

Corporal Jack featured a dog – was a dog in fact, but there was a large cast of carefully thought-out humans. The book was selling nicely and had just gone into paperback. American Cable TV was interested. My editor, the chairman's wife, Marjory Chapman, listened to my eager account of the new book on the telephone, having rung to find out how I was getting on. I was telling her that I planned to disable poor Ben, perhaps in an accident. 'But where's the dog?' she asked. When I said, 'There isn't a dog,' she told me to add one to the story in a prominent capacity if Collins was to publish the book. I had no idea at the time how publishers direct their authors along the same track when following up a successful book.

I didn't think at all when I said, 'All right, I'll blind my bloody hero and give him a guide dog.'

'Lovely idea, you do that,' said Marjory and hung up.

It was a conversation that shunted my life here and there over a long time and still does. When I'd recovered my temper, I found that I liked the idea. It involved research, visits to the Irish Guide Dogs in Cork and the rewriting of 20,000 words. When I'd spent about three months sorting out the research, I began to write again, hardly stopping until the last chapter was finished.

It was amazing how things fell into place and I think it shows that there is some answer to every problem in writing a book, something that will set the mechanism moving again, so that it can be finished in time. The first quarter of the book took much longer to write than all the rest, even allowing time for research.

5. BIRTH OF A BOOK

I've gone into this at length because I want to show not only what happened, but why and how it happened. To a lesser degree this sudden unblocking happened in both my other published novels. Perhaps it will again if I ever retrieve my most recent novel from the back burner.

You can construct a character by choosing a suitable person and accentuating some points slightly. I've done this a lot. You must be careful of course, or you might end up in court, but there are plenty of tricks to prevent that happening.

Say for example that someone you know or knew fairly well, but who wasn't a close friend, had some memorable tricks of speech, which you thought would be useful. It should be enough to alter the person's age, appearance and occupation. But even if you change their sex as well, there's still plenty there to build a fresh character.

They say that first novels are autobiographic. Mine certainly wasn't. But a scene crept in near the beginning, which I found easy to write and effective. Pleased, I read it through and realized I'd used a scene out of my own life, including my own words and those of the other person. It gave me a strange feeling, but I left it alone.

A well-drawn character can sometimes begin to 'take over' a novel, insisting on extra scenes and resisting others. Agatha did this and, like the old woman in the earlier story, continued to influence the other characters from the grave, when I'd finally nerved myself to dispose of her.

PART ONE: FICTION

Plot and storyline (see also chapters 8 and 9)

It's not easy to advise about plot or storyline. You should, of course, write an outline of your book as a guide and refer back to it as you write. A publisher needs a synopsis and a couple of chapters as a rule, but a synopsis is different as it concerns only the central plot and characters in the story, divided into a time, a place, and giving a few lines at most to each important character. I've written synopses to refer to for my own work, but haven't yet managed to keep within the confines of one. If your book needs to take on a new direction, you shouldn't stop it because you might spoil the look of the synopsis. Don't constrain your imagination any more than you need.

If your key characters are well portrayed and develop as they should, part of the plotline may be in opposition to them. One or the other has to be rethought and rewritten. The synopsis, for choice.

Big, blockbuster-style books demand plots to match. Hosts of characters, half a dozen subplots, shifts in time and location. You may feel you have a blockbuster in you (sounds uncomfortable), but I'd be inclined to leave it there. I'd hesitate to write one unless begged to by a rich, dependable publisher with a six-figure advance in mind. Even then, I wouldn't be happy about it. It's not an activity I recommend to the part-timer.

For a middle-of-the-road quality novel you need a storyline carried mainly by your two to four principal characters, one of whom is in opposition to the others. I don't mean the good old eternal triangle, necessarily, but the challenge present

5. BIRTH OF A BOOK

in almost all fiction. Teachers of creative writing usually call this 'conflict' and I don't really like the term. But yes, your key character should be in conflict with somebody or something.

A plot is hard to define. It forms a narrative into a beginning, a middle, and an end. It keeps you reading.

6. Dialogue

I've talked about making characters 'live' and shown that it isn't a matter of detailed description so much as entering into their minds and seeing through their eyes. You make your character eat, sleep, walk about, suffer; feel happiness, love, hate, fear – all the emotions that go to build a three-dimensional thinking person. But many beginners, while they can manage all this, stop short at making the character speak.

I judged twelve stories for beginner writers in a competition some years back, and was amazed to find that, in exactly half, there was no dialogue at all. Now, by muzzling your characters and making them act their parts in silence, you are giving yourself an unnecessary handicap. Emotions bring characters to life and speech expresses emotion. Your key character looks, moves, feels – you must allow him to speak.

Some beginners, apparently afraid of dialogue, take refuge

6. DIALOGUE

in reported speech. I think this is a result of listening to the news and current affairs on TV. 'The president said that …', 'An Taoiseach agreed that …' Reported speech, as I'm sure you know, tells what was said indirectly. It has its place in a narrative, especially when a conversation needs to be compressed, and to cut down on repetition. This sort of conversation might occur in a crime story, where it is essential for the matter to be discussed, perhaps by a number of people. It can be inserted into a conversation, when somebody who hasn't been speaking joins a group, so as to show that here is a different voice. Ordinarily though, reported speech lacks life. Given at length, it may also result in some strangely structured sentences.

'Jill said she thought it would be a good idea to go out for a drink, as she had been talking to Margaret and Margaret had said they might meet, but Joan had said that …' I could go on.

'Let's go to Doyle's,' said Jill. 'Margaret said she'd be there.' This is simpler, more real and much more interesting. Note the naming of the pub and the brief, positive phrasing. Journalists habitually make use of reported speech, as it can be conveniently vague when necessary. At times, it's unwise to quote directly. Attempts to quote VIPs verbatim must be backed up by a recording, so as to avert furious denials and lawsuits. Reported speech also edits, picking out the central meaning, if any.

Whatever your line of country, you must learn to write good dialogue. First you plan your story, then you populate it. Finally you write it, and that's where dialogue comes in.

PART ONE: FICTION

Experience will teach you where and when to use it. I will try to explain why we use it.

Dialogue makes characters live

You can show what they are really like through their speech more effectively than by minute descriptions. Example: 'Jack was a mean man. Every penny was accounted for, he was stingy with the housekeeping. He never went on holiday or bought a present for Jill. His substantial win in the National Lottery had been cautiously invested with Amalgamated Sewer Pipes.' There's nothing actually wrong with this, but it doesn't really get into Jack's head or show how he appeared to others.

With dialogue, you will hear Jack telling somebody what a bargain he got in the charity shop, 'Had to haggle of course, got 50 cents off ...' or boasting that he's never yet paid for a bus ticket in the city.

Dialogue makes a story real

Jack's comment shows that aspect too. A discussion is more real than a description. I don't mean that you should write reams of dialogue where it isn't needed, but when you use it to 'round' a character, it should be brief.

6. DIALOGUE

Dialogue advances the plot

This is important. Every line of dialogue you write should carry your story forward. If it doesn't, think before you put it in. Descriptive dialogue advances the plot because it develops the characters and background, which are part of the progress of the story. Conversation can be used to bridge time. You leave your characters saying goodbye to their hosts, then, after a break, their conversation may show that it is now a week later and they are in a different country. This is a handy trick in a short story of 1000 words or less, but usually out of place in a novel.

Dialogue indicates the emotional state of the speaker

Jack is frightened. You describe his appearance and actions and this may suffice if your descriptive powers are good. If they are only moderate, try making him show us how frightened he is.

'Jack's face was chalk white. "Don't go in there, Jill."

"Why not?" asked Jill, taking another step forward.

"Never mind why not – " Jack's voice shook. "I'm asking you, Jill …" he struggled to control his voice …'

These lines are more effective than description.

Dialogue increases pace

This may sound like nonsense. It may hold up the action, but it shouldn't.

Consider: 'Jane looked up and saw that the tree was about to fall. She shouted a warning to Mike.'

Now try: 'Jane looked up. "Look out, Mike. The tree's coming down!" she yelled.'

This reminds me of another point. People don't normally use one another's names every time they speak.

'It's raining, Jack.'

'Is it, Jill?'

'Yes, Jack.'

They do use names in moments of stress, emotion or fear.

'I love you, Jack.'

'I love you too, Jill.'

Americans tend to break this rule, with a constant using of names.

Dialogue breaks up the page into readable short paragraphs

From a commercial point of view, dialogue has a cosmetic value. Readers enjoy reading it and editors print what readers want. Whenever you start a sentence in quotes, you open a new paragraph, unless the same speaker continues to talk following a break. Even for a plain 'Yes' or 'No' you should, strictly speaking, use a fresh line. Experienced writers bend this rule, but beginners are advised to leave rule-bending alone for the present.

Good dialogue makes a narrative pacier, more immediate, more authentic. Bad dialogue slows it up and bores the reader, who recognizes padding when he sees it. It is possible to write a short story entirely in dialogue, although I don't advise it. Generally speaking, the more literary the story, the less chat – there are exceptions of course. Dialogue, being nearer to life than description, is easier to read; those reared on TV and comics feel daunted by long chunks of text. This is one of the reasons why old-fashioned schoolbooks are so difficult to read today.

A lightweight story with a fragile plot will get by with sparkling, witty dialogue and minimal narration. Please don't use dialogue to try to salvage a shaky plot unless you are sure that it *is* sparkling and witty. Ask the opinion of a friend with a sense of humour.

Dialogue should be natural, pointed, consistent

Don't bow too much to realism. If you listen to conversations on the average city bus, you won't learn much about dialogue. The weather – gruesome disease – football –babies – the weather again, and a mind-numbing lack of imagination in the use of obscenities. Still, if you were to record all this, you might be able to edit some of it into publishable dialogue. You must take the vital parts of a conversation and dump the rest, leaving out all the repetition, the ers and ahs and you knows. It is usually necessary to make dialogue more pointed and tidier than in real life. If you are tempted to write in dialect, do resist temptation.

Phonetic spelling and stage Irish are out of fashion and extremely hard to do successfully. I had a lot of trouble with Yorkshire dialect in *No Harp Like My Own*, and only included it because a particular character would have spoken in that way and no other. It is not for the novice. Similarly, an Irish person's phrasing is as distinctive as his pronunciation. It's generally enough.

I upset one of Collins' staff with a bit of Yorkshire. 'The Guvnor', approaching Ben's guide dog, enquires, 'Awd bitch bite? She better hadn't.' I'd heard this phrase in Yorkshire and liked it. It came back to me as, 'Does the old bitch bite? She'd better not.' I changed it back and they let it go.

In a contemporary story, you should avoid fashionable catchwords, which are likely to be dead in a few months. Slang is all right. Use the formal 'cannot' and 'will not' for emphasis only. 'I cannot and I will not do your dirty work for you.' For general use, stick to 'can't' and 'won't'.

Now for the 'he said', 'she said' bit. An overworked word, but I stick to 'said' because it is unobtrusive. You should make it obvious who is speaking, so you need use it only occasionally. You can vary 'said' with 'replied', 'snapped', 'whispered' and so on as appropriate, but please avoid eye-catching horrors such as 'gurgled', 'snorted', 'gushed', 'opined'. These verbs attract the reader's attention away from *what* was said.

6. DIALOGUE

In order to show who is speaking without 'said', introduce action. 'Jack drew his chair up to the table. "I'm starving."

Jill placed a pie in front of him. "I'm afraid the pastry isn't great."'

Talking of pastry, a heavy hand with dialogue is rather like a heavy hand with pastry. ' "Oh, Jack," cooed Sue (or shrilled Jill). "If you do not restrict your intake of carbohydrates, I fear that problems of obesity may occur."'

Dialogue can be useful if you want to describe something and don't know how.

Okay. You wish to describe a new baby, but you have never examined one closely. 'Laura peeped ecstatically into the folds of blue wool. "Isn't he perfect? Isn't he gorgeous?" she breathed.' Cheating like this is easy when you get the knack of it.

Here's another example: fashion is a closed book to you, but you want to describe a perfectly dressed woman. For the purpose of the narrative, you must. 'She was perfectly dressed' has nothing going for it. Neither has 'She was dressed in some clinging white stuff.' Nor, 'She wore a chic costume in purple.'

Here's the trick. You make another woman say, 'Oh, Miriam, you look fantastic. Where did you find that dress?' The reader doesn't even know the colour of the outfit, but is left with the required impression – a perfectly dressed woman.

This sneaky trick can be used for any area unfamiliar to the writer, from abstract art to aero engines.

Adverbs are useful for shortening the text, but shortening and increasing pace are not the same thing. You should avoid

PART ONE: FICTION

long adverbs. I have selected a few from the stories in a short-story competition I judged.

> Abstractedly
> Belligerently
> Categorically
> Disconsolately
> Magnificently
> Unceremoniously

Here are some shorter synonyms:

> Vaguely
> Fiercely
> Flatly
> Sadly
> Grandly
> Informally

They mean the same as the first batch, as near as dammit, and to my mind they are more effective. Use adverbs selectively, and leave them out unless it is necessary to know how the person spoke.

Vary your dialogue with action and natural pauses – remember that you aim to write natural-sounding conversation.

Finally, judge what you've written by reading it aloud to yourself. This goes for all writing, but especially for dialogue. It's as simple as that. What looks okay written down, can sound impossible. Try saying each sentence aloud before writing it down. Even now, I often do the reading test. It's the

6. DIALOGUE

best tip I can give you. As an editor, I often read a sentence that is almost right, but not quite. I read it aloud and at once the fault is plain to see – or rather, hear.

7. Usage and Abusage

(*With apologies to the ghost of Eric Partridge, whose book title this was.*)

When I read the work of beginner writers, I am often struck by their fondness for flashback.

In short fiction there is no place for flashback and it's never an easy way to write. If you follow my suggestion and start with something eye-catching you should go on from there, not back. 'Mary woke with a scream.' Okay, you've got my attention. But if you go on, 'She lived in a three bed roomed, semi-detached bungalow, in a suburb of a market town in the south, left to her by a relative some years previously', you are well on the way to losing it again. If you continue in this vein for a page or more, you are going to have trouble linking up with that scream, which is where we came

7. USAGE & ABUSAGE

in. You should tell us why Mary screamed, the reader wants to know, and will probably skip if not told. Then give us some action, and if possible some dialogue.

If you must use flashback, you are obliged to use the past perfect tense, at least until the time is established. She had inherited, she had lived – the straight past tense is wrong here. So, start at the beginning and go on to the end. It's easier for you as well as for the reader. Action that has taken place before the opening of the story is best given by way of dialogue or through a character's thoughts. 'Sometimes Mary wished Uncle Tom hadn't left her the house. It was much too big, and anyway she hated the country.' A huge house? The thought could have occurred to Mary as she padded down five flights of stairs to investigate whatever it was that made her scream.

These remarks mainly apply to short stories, but flashback is a difficult option in a novel. I started *Corporal Jack* with a flash-forward, so to speak, and this is quite an effective ploy. You show something of importance, which makes the reader want to know what went before. You then work towards it from an earlier scene. In this case, the flash-forward was to the trenches of World War 1 and I used it because the true beginning of the book, which set up the story, was essential but not riveting. At the end of the first chapter, I did a second flash-forward, connecting with the earlier one. I think the device worked but, as I've said, it isn't the easiest to do.

As for non-fiction, there is no place at all for flashback there. You must restrain your stylistic flourishes when the content is what matters.

PART ONE: FICTION

Style

Style is a personal thing. It comes to you with practice, developing along with your imagination. You cultivate it as you do your memory. Style starts with the way you speak, so it's an advantage if you speak good English naturally. Speak natural, unforced prose and with luck you will write it too. You might think that English teachers would make the best writers, but this isn't the case. The most correct perhaps, but that's another matter altogether.

Your computer may correct your spelling with a red wiggly line and your grammar with a green one. Be careful though and don't feel you must obey its instructions every time. I'm grateful when it picks up the hundreds of typos I commit when I hurry, but it also 'corrects' idiosyncrasies of style. My style is my own and yours is yours. We don't need Windows XP to regularize it.

You mustn't copy consciously, although most of us copy unconsciously. If you need a model, choose a top writer of today, not yesterday. The classics are still classics: Scott, Dickens and Hardy are still read at school, but their style of writing is as dated as the clothes and manners of their era.

Translated into movies, they can succeed brilliantly. Dickens' classics came out weekly in magazines, thickly plotted, full of the immediate concerns of their time and with each instalment ending with a cliff-hanger. Sometimes a fairly low cliff … but he did make them last … today all that closely printed bulk puts us off, as does the sickly sentiment. Strong men have wept manly tears over the death of little Nell; today's readers are made of sterner stuff.

7. USAGE & ABUSAGE

Oddly enough, Victorian children were often regaled with tales of torture, burnings alive and disembowelling. As a child, I read Harrison Ainsworth's *Old St Paul's*, and have remembered the last scene ever since. In it, the villain and his wife, thinking themselves safe from the great fire of London in the crypt of St Paul's, watch in horror and disbelief as the lead off the roof appears, melted and boiling, under their door and advances across the floor. I had nightmares about it.

The works of great writers of the past have survived because of their gifts of inventiveness, originality and wit. They have been copied so often that they are no longer relevant, and their humour is out of date. Only inventiveness is left, and that was personal to them. And don't forget that a copy of what bored you at school will bore other readers today. A generation brought up on television won't sit still and read a long description – or not unless it is marvellously well done.

A new generation of school-goers has read Henry James, Graham Greene, Ernest Hemingway; even Wodehouse and Waugh. This was an advance, but still not a great deal of help to the aspiring writer in the twenty-first century. Now, there are newer titles on the school reading lists, such as *To Kill a Mocking Bird* and *The Catcher in the Rye*. Even these have been around for thirty or forty years. The schools take a long time to catch up. Then they astonish us by including Cecelia Ahern's *PS I Love You* on the reading list.

Some descriptive narrative is necessary in every story, and essential in a novel. The greater the proposed length, the higher will be the proportion of direct narrative. Most of us

PART ONE: FICTION

learn to narrate – it's what we did in our school essays – that's why I've been insisting on other ways of telling a story, using the character's eyes and minds to convey information to the reader. Now, I propose to deal with narrative and description, which is what most beginners choose to write, and is one of the hardest things to do successfully without some guidance.

Never be tedious; a description should be as interesting as anything else in your book and it will be if you study it, for it is one of the things in fiction writing that you can learn to do better, with rules to improve your technique and train your mind. It is an opportunity to use those long words, but only where they are exactly what you need. Check some out in the thesaurus. Narrative comes after plot, character and dialogue because you must have something relevant and important to your plot to describe.

Let's say that you would like to describe a thunderstorm. You get it right with your growling, crackling prose; if you were writing an essay, it would get top marks. But if it isn't an integral part of your story, it will hold up the action instead of advancing it. A thunderstorm portrayed by a hidden narrator is of interest only to him or her.

Say you are sold on that thunderstorm. You have written 500 words of vivid description. Let it occur so as to affect the action, the protagonist watches in horror as the lightning strikes ... now you can show it as well as telling it. Your nicely chosen words should be thought by a literate character, not by someone who would merely wonder if the split and scorched tree was going to block his way home.

Narrative is useful when you need to break up a scene without being sudden and brutal about it. Used wisely, it doesn't show any joins. Don't forget that straight narrative, written without an observer within the book, still needs to be told from a viewpoint. So when you describe, imagine, hear and see what you are describing.

Keep it simple

Good writing appears simple, even when the writer has studied every word with care. It should be easier to write simply than to adorn your work with redundant words. It isn't. Few writers achieve simplicity allied with originality except after years of practice. The unnecessary or ill-chosen adjective is the enemy of simplicity. Omitting adjectives without losing readability is an art.

Your meaning should always be clear, and in dialogue, there should never be any doubt about who is speaking. When the narrative flows, it's readable. It should never be jerky or clumsy. Beware of tricks, obscure analogies and facetiousness. All these things are you, the writer, obscuring the subject. When you are published, successful, sure of yourself, you can fiddle about with stylistic experiments. Until then, only do so for your own amusement.

Your style should be influenced by your subject. For violent action and excitement, short sentences, short paragraphs, minimum description. For romance, or a gentle theme, a different vocabulary, a smoother flow of words. A simple style for a simple story, something more elaborate for a complicated theme. It may seem unlikely, but many new writers produce elaborate work because they haven't learned to write simple English. If you are to be an efficient writer, capable of turning out saleable fiction, you must be able to vary pace and decide how much trimming to give your basic narrative.

This is the foundation to build on. The foundation might be the launching pad for a career as a best-selling novelist, a high-powered journalist or a distinguished author of memoirs or biographies. First, you develop your own style, then you learn to modify it. If you want your readers to laugh and cry, you must vary your style, sometimes from one page to the next.

When I turn to non-fiction I will show how working as a reporter helps a writer to learn when and what to discard. The new fiction writer is often over-sensitive and protective of his work. When he learns how sub-editors treat copy they don't care for, he either makes a decision to write only what will pass muster or gives up in despair.

The cliché

At a workshop I held, an argument developed about Shakespeare. Mind you, arguments are the lifeblood of workshops; without them, apathy sets in, unless the tutors are truly inspired. The lady who was leading the anti-Shakespeare faction, declared that he wrote in clichés – and I had been telling her to avoid these whenever possible. As proof, she produced an article she'd cut out of a writers' magazine, with one example after another. ' "Sleep like a top,"' she said. 'What's that but a cliché?'

As I tried to explain that Shakespeare's now hackneyed phrases were new-minted when he used them, it occurred to me that fresh clichés appear all the time, but we don't recognize them. They are witty epigrams or nicely turned phrases when they are first used. Let me use a cliché, hailed as a witty quip some years ago, and say that they have passed their sell-by date.

The cliché is the biggest single enemy of good writing: the overworked phrase that comes into every writer's mind, offering a short cut. There are three main types. One is the topical catchphrase used by politicians, for example 'at this moment in time' (it means now). Then there is the tired simile: as cold as ice, as black as ink, as hungry as a hunter. Try to think up a few fresh similes of your own. The others are stale. Next comes the over-quoted quote: 'dirty work at the crossroads', 'an eye to the main chance', 'something nasty in the woodshed'.

It is impossible to cut cliché out of your work entirely. I noticed when reading what I'd written at the beginning of this book that I referred to a busy housewife. You may say, 'Yes, housewives are busy.' What, all of them? We all know this isn't the case. I wrote the words without thinking. Many clichés, now used all the time, are metaphors that once made somebody pause and say, 'That's clever!' A cliché is a dead metaphor, proverb or epigram.

PART ONE: FICTION

Journalists are especially at risk, as a careful use of cliché gives a sort of comforting familiarity to work aimed at a not too fussy readership. Writing quickly, to a deadline, encourages journalists to cut corners and few editors object.

Jargon, which is used in almost all journalism, is found in specialized reporting, especially sporting headlines. Racehorse trot home, football teams are annihilated, pulverized or are glorious in defeat. This kind of thing usually goes unnoticed by the reader – who is interested in sport rather than fine writing.

In fact, many stock phrases are expected and would be missed. Some of the phrases creep into the language and into works of fiction. In this way, words lose their original meaning and are given another. 'Petrify' means turn to stone, not terrify. 'Literally' suffers even worse abuse. 'I was literally rooted to the ground.'

Such misused words, if not exactly clichés, are chosen in a hurry without thought for their meaning. I give a list of some of the ones I hate most later on.

If you invent a character who calls his wife 'his better half', and his drink 'the cup that cheers' or 'what the doctor ordered', then let him. At once, you call up a picture of an old-fashioned pompous person, lacking a sense of humour. It is you, as narrator, who must guard against cliché, to avoid attaching the pompous, humourless label to yourself.

Euphemism

Many euphemisms have become clichés. These are cosy little phrases that dress up such basic realities as death in comforting words. Pass away, pass on, go home – slangily, kick the bucket. They may be used in dialogue, but in narrative a character should simply die. There are euphemisms for every bodily function. Some are acceptable, even necessary, some are not. If you invent a character that thinks and speaks in this way, okay, let him, but you, as narrator, should remove dishonesty from your work, except when the alternative would be offensive.

To hear clichés at their most banal, listen to someone forced at short notice to make a speech. 'Unaccustomed as I am to public speaking,' he starts and presently refers to somebody's advice to 'stand up, speak up and shut up'. He will mention the happy pair (wedding), sad occasion (funeral), and refer to the kindness or otherwise of the weather (garden fête).

What is the effect of such a speech? The answer is that it has none, because nobody ever listens. Each sentence begun can be mentally finished off by the audience. Friends of the speaker can be relied on to laugh or clap in the right places, others follow suit.

Similarly, written clichés have no impact because they aren't read. Readers may run their eyes over them but, as with the speech, they are well ahead of the writer and can finish off the sentences themselves.

Adjectives

A 'lazy' adjective is a clichéd adjective. The presence or absence of clichés highlights the difference between popular and literary writing. Just as the sporting press has its own expected catchphrases, you will find others in thrillers, romances and most kinds of genre fiction. Good middle-of-the-road fiction uses only those that are fresh enough to add to the impact of the story. The literary perfectionist, who polishes each phrase to its starkly simple best, is setting him or herself a difficult task. It can be done, but unless new similes and metaphors are included, the result can be like an unfurnished room.

I should mention here that literary fiction can surprise and delight you with a turn of phrase or a happy choice of adjective. It can make you think, make you wait impatiently for the author's next book. One reason that keeps it out of the popular bracket is that it may well lack the touch of sentiment latent in most people.

I think it was Ruth Rendell who used the simile 'as cold as clay' of a corpse. Turning the page, ready to read the word, 'ice', 'clay' made me pause. Certainly many things are neither warmer nor colder than clay, but used of a dead hand, the alternative, with its macabre overtones held a hint of menace that 'ice' would have lacked.

Clichés need to be cut out of your writing, but don't attempt too much surgery as you go along. It can be disheartening and make you lose the thread of the narrative.

Do the reading aloud test if in doubt. When that is done

7. USAGE & ABUSAGE

and some editing, you should have a piece of work that will demand to be read with attention.

Returning to those lazy adjectives, don't forget that the purpose of an adjective is to qualify a noun. This may be a matter of necessity, when description demands that we use them, or they may serve to make the narrative different and more stylish. To serve either purpose, they should be fresh and interesting. If they aren't, they take away from the nouns qualified instead of adding to them. 'Nice' and 'pretty' are examples of weak adjectives. They have no power except when used sarcastically: 'You made a "nice" or "pretty" mess of that.'

Some writers specialize in adjectives, stringing two or three together with evident pleasure. Iris Murdoch was an example. But hers was a love affair with words. When our achievements match hers, we will be entitled to experiment. A quote comes to mind. '… his [or more probably her] long, pale, passionate face …' It sounds like Murdoch but may not be. These words must have been well chosen in their context, or I'd have forgotten them a long time ago. Some writers, seeking to make their descriptions poetic, would have rearranged the words. '… her face was long, passionate, pale.' This kind of mannerism can be effective when used sparingly, and extremely tedious when overdone.

Seeking to amuse my students in Nenagh when one asked what I meant by multiple adjectives in a sentence, I said, 'Tall, Protestant, bad-tempered Marjorie was wearing …' I didn't get any farther because the words worked. They were amusing

PART ONE: FICTION

and were remembered, as I intended them to be. Another point about simple readability is that active is almost always better than passive. I could as easily have written just now, 'as they were intended to be'. Beginners often go passive ('The post had been collected by Amy') and it is an unnecessary twisting of words. Word-twisting won't work if you want to be simple. 'Amy had collected the post.'

For straight, unadorned yet hard-hitting prose, I recommend the Gospels. The parables were told for the most part to uneducated fishermen and farmers, in the simplest of terms. The subjects were mundane – a lost sheep, a dishonest workman, a failed crop. Yet, those stories, told without frills, have lived for two thousand years and I suggest that those who sneer at their simplicity should try writing a few parables themselves. Most are free of adjectives except those that are essential.

I am not so disingenuous as to suggest that literary style alone has made the Gospels live. They, like Shakespeare, were translated at a time when the English language was extremely beautiful. The bowdlerized, one-size-fits-all versions of today have lost out in that they are no longer memorable. Something valuable has gone.

When I was a child, a relative sent me a book by Scott or Dickens every birthday and Christmas. The books were viciously abridged to about an eighth of their original length and the series was called: 'The Classics, Told to the Bairns'. You lose something – you gain something. Accessibility, I suppose, is good, but the books didn't survive their generation.

7. USAGE & ABUSAGE

Many beginners are tempted to write 'purple prose', littered with adjectives, most of them metaphorical. 'Brooding mountains'. 'Weeping clouds'. 'Agonizing hours'. These examples are also called pathetic fallacy, or making nature agree with the mood of the writer. I have wondered at the sudden eruptions of overwrought prose in some new writers' work, blaming it on a diet of Victorian poets in our formative years. Yet I believe there is another reason: the instinct to hide from recognition and the inhibitions that beset new writers, who hedge themselves round with over-embellished sentences.

I've mentioned the twin worries of the embryo writer: the fear that we won't be read and the fear that we will be. When we put something of ourselves into our writing to make it live, that means self-revelation. It's natural to dive back into your shell, to hide behind an excess of adjectives.

When I started writing fiction I sailed along without worrying until the plot demanded something deeply personal and emotional. I then stopped and left that bit for later. When I returned to it, I took refuge in a shallow jokey style, which gave nothing away. This was my chosen form of escape, because I was a humorous writer first and a novelist second. When I'm frightened, embarrassed or upset, I make jokes – it's an instinctive means of defence – just as I did at boarding school. Playing the clown and hiding behind a wall of words was a shield – of sorts.

Finally, having chosen the adjective that is exactly right, do remember to put it in the right place. There are plenty of examples, such as 'For sale, three green bridesmaid's dresses', which appeared in the local press … green bridesmaids?

As far as possible, avoid using the word 'very'. It is so common that it has lost its power. 'It was very cold' is hardly stronger than 'It was a cold night'. Use it for emphasis like this: 'Are you cold?' 'Yes, very.' You should look for a strong single adjective to replace a weak one qualified by 'very'. It is another example of lazy description. Other qualifying adverbs are 'quite', 'rather', 'fairly'. You will need to use these and others from time to time, but they muzzle your prose, making it cautious and uncertain. Journalists in particular should try not to sound uncertain.

Pace and directness are important and irrelevancies should go. Get what you have to say down on paper, and then cut and trim where necessary.

Closely related to cliché is tautology, or the use of two or more synonymous words to describe something. 'At once' and 'immediately' in the same sentence is an example, or 'a huge, big man'. Choose the stronger adjective of the two, i.e. huge.

Allied to this is the blinding glimpse of the obvious. It is not necessary to say that your hero wore an old school tie round his neck. If it was knotted round his head or carried between his teeth it would be remarkable, otherwise, the three words 'round his neck' are redundant and should be omitted. There are scores of examples of this kind of thing. 'She poured the tea into the cup' – not down the sink or out of the window. 'She poured out the tea' will suffice. 'Into the cup' should be left out unless the actual tea pouring is a significant part of the plot, for example if the cup already contained poison.

Padding

This is the fault that irritates editors and publishers to screaming point: an effort to stretch a story to the required length by adding inessentials. Your options here are to write a shorter story or to introduce a fresh incident. *Never* write a sentence like this: 'They boarded the 8.40 train in Nenagh, after a short wait, the train being only a few minutes late, and arrived at Ballybrophy at 9.30 without incident.' Exact time is seldom significant except in crime writing. Anyway, this is an utterly negative sentence. It implies that the norm was a train robbery at Cloughjordan or a hijacking at Roscrea. It suggests that a collision with the Cork express was mercifully avoided. It's padding. 'They went to Ballybrophy by train that morning' should be enough for anybody.

Rules of grammar

My knowledge of formal grammar is almost nil. This might seem like a good reason for not writing a book of this kind. My grammar is instinctive. Good reading helps.

But in a writer, ignorance of grammar is not a disaster, a mild handicap perhaps, like difficulty with spelling. In fact it may be better if you don't know too many rules; it may help you to develop a feeling for words, a sense of the rightness or otherwise of a phrase, which is a personal thing.

One or two issues have struck me, which I should mention. 'In the door' and 'out the door' are incorrect without the addition of *through*, *of*, or *at*. 'Through the door' is all right, although it might suggest having to use a saw. You can avoid meeting this one head on by saying merely, 'came in' or 'went out'.

'All right' is supposed to be two separate words, not as in 'already' or 'although'. 'Alright' is American in origin, but is now common elsewhere. 'Okay' is usually spelt 'okay' rather than 'OK'. These aren't really rules and both alternatives are gradually becoming acceptable and being absorbed into the language. Again, most Irish writers ignore these rules, as do most Americans.

Good English

This reads better than bad, but what is it? It certainly isn't cumbersome speech following a set of rules. Write natural English. Write as you speak. Try not to make grammatical errors in your narrative, but they will be edited if your work is published. It takes more than an ill-placed preposition to condemn a story. Forget the rules you learned as a child, you aren't at school, so don't write as if you were. Strive to write English that sounds correct by all means, but if a sentence sounds stilted or unnatural, while being grammatical, do try to tweak it into a more acceptable form.

Some of the English that we learned at school tried to weed out our Irish constructions. Leave them in. There was never anything wrong with being an Irish writer – quite the opposite – so don't be ashamed of writing like one. The errors to be avoided are usages like, 'He suggested that John and me should go too', or 'He gave the keys to John and I'. Both are incorrect. The way to tell is to link the subject with the second person named. That would give you, 'He gave the keys to I' and 'He suggested that me should go too'. This makes the mistake obvious. He gave the keys to me. These examples are of bad grammar as well as bad English.

'John took his time getting the messages' may be incorrect, but it doesn't make you wince. You know that John is Irish, that's all.

So many Irish people are natural storytellers and we are known for it worldwide. Yet the commonest fault with beginner writers, here and elsewhere, is to tie down the narrative, slow it up and explain too much. J.B. Keane, Alice Taylor, Frank McCourt and Roddy Doyle all tell a story when writing a novel. Their voices come through the written words, telling so that we listen. This is because they are natural storytellers and draw the reader in, as the *seanchaí* draws his audience to gather round and listen. We get the feeling that we are listening rather than reading.

Writing as you speak should be simple and it makes for easy reading, provided that that you are a good talker.

Punctuation

My punctuation, like my grammar, is instinctive. You must think of it as being like the Sabbath – made for man, not the reverse. Some writers try to do without it, except for full stops. This isn't a good idea.

PART ONE: FICTION

Brilliant American novelist Cormac McCarthy gets away with it most of the time, but which of us has his technique? He also manages nicely without quotes. Roddy Doyle favours dashes instead of quotes, a convention adopted by Joyce from French usage.

A comma indicates a slight pause, and also the meaning. 'She loses her breath and pants' without a comma, suggests missing underwear. This example also gives the lie to the rule that a comma should *never* precede the word 'and'. I've been bending this rule for so long that I often forget it, but surely one can make an informed change? I'm told that this bastard sign inserted before 'and' is called an 'Oxford comma'. I couldn't find it in the Oxford dictionary, so I will leave it to writers' common sense.

Linking two unrelated things, as in 'breath' and 'pants', usually done for comic effect, is called 'zeugma', a splendid word for Scrabble players.

Read your work aloud, I repeat. This exercise will tell you where the commas should go. Punctuation is slanted at reading aloud, whether you notice it or not. Don't forget to use a question mark when appropriate, and go easy on the exclamation marks. These may be used in dialogue – 'I've lost my ticket!' – but I don't like them in narrative. They draw the writer in, offering his comments. Dashes are useful in dialogue, I use them more than I should, I think. They are a good alternative to brackets. Dots, which are called ellipses, come in handy too, when somebody's voice tails off, or a sentence is left unfinished.

Putting a dash instead of a swear word is unfashionable, but beginners still do it, especially older ones. Write whatever it is in full, or leave it out if you prefer, being a sensitive soul. You can mention that the person's conversation was peppered with oaths, and leave them to the reader's imagination. Dashes for place-names are a Victorian conceit, now obsolete.

Description

Describe what matters to the people or the plot. Don't put in description because you're good at it, save your talents for the places where the narrative requires a scene to be set. Then be careful, because poor description is what makes readers skip.

Avoid long sentences. These are the hallmark of the beginner. Long paragraphs fill the page and daunt the reader, long sentences confuse him.

'The rays of the sinking sun shone through the pines which grew on the mossy slope which led down to the shore of the little lake which nestled in a fold of the hills which …' Remove at least two 'whiches' [the first two should be 'that' anyhow, being defining clauses – *ed*.] and think of a better word than 'nestled'. Try to think up some similes of your own, and don't forget that allowing the scenery and weather to agree with the mood of your story is in order and can add much to the atmosphere.

I myself would hesitate to describe, say, a rainbow or a sunset, because everyone knows what they look like. In fact, they are used for comparison themselves.

6. DIALOGUE

A last word about style. Either describe or don't. Never use phrases like 'and other things' 'etc.' or 'and so on'. These phrases are the thingummys and whatyermaycalls of writing. Describe as much as you need to, then stop. In dialogue, I hope you wouldn't make a character say, 'When Thingy comes, tell him I brought the yokes from town' although I have heard speech like this. Verbal and written laziness are closely related.

Some writers go to the opposite extreme. 'John returned from the metropolis with the items that he had been requested to bring.'

'When John arrives, kindly inform him that Marjorie has proceeded to the emporium and has already purchased the articles that you requested …'

There is an anecdote about Winston Churchill, when somebody was talking to the great man about his latest book. This person said, '… but you should never end a sentence with a preposition.' Churchill replied, 'This is the kind of arrant pedantry up with which I will not put.'

Read it aloud …

8. Narrative and Construction

I've written about narrative in a general way. Of course there is plenty more to be said, but first you need to know more about the construction, both of a short story and of a novel. Novels are as long as you care to make them within generous limits; the themes, plots and general layout are up to the writer, except in the case of genre fiction.

The average novel is around 80,000 to 100,000 words long. It may be as short as 35,000 words and if you are a Hemingway or an Orwell, you might get away with that. Otherwise you stand a better chance of publication with 65,000 words or more. A 'blockbuster' may run to 200,000 words. But you are a beginner. Approaching a publisher with a manuscript a foot thick is just a waste of time. The cost of production wouldn't justify a gamble on a promising beginner.

PART ONE: FICTION

A successful novelist may do this kind of thing after a time.

Short stories are another matter. When you write one with a purpose, whether for a magazine, a competition or for radio, you will be confined to a certain length or reading time. Most short stories are from 600 to 2000 words long. There are sites on the Internet that will keep you informed of all the short-story competitions going. I suggest that you look out for those within your scope and give it a go. Some allow you to send your competition by e-mail attachment, but most don't. Check that you are eligible; there's often small print that disqualifies some entries. Some competitions are free to enter. When there's a fee, it's generally quite small.

There are hundreds that you can enter and they are excellent practice. Two people who attended a course that I held won prizes; both were surprised. One lady got a first in an Irish contest; another was second in a prestigious competition in England.

Do be careful to follow the rules. An outstanding story will win without comment if the others are moderate, but in a close finish judges start by checking that the winner has read the small print. I have been in that position myself, as judge. Two stories out of almost a hundred stood out and I read both twice, still unable to separate them, although they were unalike. Finally, I decided that the one that followed the theme given, making it central to the story, should beat the other, of equal merit, which mentioned the word in the title and maybe once thereafter. I felt that the story might easily have been offered at any competition, with a different title,

8. NARRATIVE AND CONSTRUCTION

while the other matched the requirements and was plainly written for the contest.

This is an area when rules of construction are important. The entry forms show what type of story is wanted. Sometimes a first or last line is provided, sometimes a subject. The publication or group that has set the competition is a reliable guide as to whether your entry should be literary, popular or traditional.

A 'literary' story gives more latitude in that it is formed by the writer for effect. Yes, it can be written along the same lines as any other, but there is far more room for indulging yourself as you write. It's more important to be on the same wavelength as the judge than in a plotted story, whose framework is given to you ready-made.

Popular and traditional stories are made up in roughly the same way, having an identifiable plot, a beginning, a middle and an ending, plus believable characters who act in believable ways. You also need a climax in the telling, after which the plot quickly winds down to the ending. Constructing your story exactly as specified is an obvious way to gain a head start.

When you write for a magazine, you should study its readership and editorial style. Be prepared for rejections for a variety of reasons. I have sent material to a number of magazines, receiving courteous replies, but few acceptances.

The cheaper type of popular magazine may well buy most of its stories from agencies. I discovered this when by chance I met a man in the business of grooming stories for different markets. Names of places are altered, spelling changed for America, often they are translations. When you send in a story, you get first serial rights. Always mark your work copyright, adding your name and the date. With magazines, the deal is 'first serial rights', meaning that you give that story to be printed once. Reprinting sometimes incurs a fee, but a much smaller one. If the story is sold to an agency, there isn't much you can do about it. To print 'copyright' ©, press C and 'Alt Gr' together on your PC, 'Option' and G on your Mac.

Never forget a title-page, which should be stapled or clipped to the first page. Put the name of the story and your own name in the centre of the page, your address in the top right-hand corner, and the date, copyright and number of words in the lower left-hand corner. This goes for everything you offer a publisher or editor.

Some stories allow you to use your imagination freely, these are usually run by writers' groups or arts' committees. When you get this chance, do use it. Don't be afraid to give it your best shot. If a good friend tells you it's politically incorrect or controversial or pessimistic, don't listen.

Are you, like me, putting character ahead of storyline? Popular stories generally show a character developing. A more literary kind, one that allows you to give free rein to your imagination, is as likely to show the character disintegrating. Try to write a positive ending though, unless the judges are young people. The younger they are, the more set they appear to be against happy endings. At least, that's been my experience. You expect energy, enthusiasm, passion, freshness, but often you get misery, disease and death.

From the elderly and downright old, you might expect informed, well-reasoned prose. Often, you get it. What you sometimes do discover is a simple joy of living that is surprising.

Writing stories for radio

Here is your chance to *tell* a story, to be a storyteller and not worry too much about punctuation. Starting with the Francis MacManus short-story competition, there are more outlets than ever before for stories on radio. As before, you should think of your audience. Mid-morning stories are often aimed at stay-at-home mums and elderly or housebound people. Afternoon radio is less likely to feature stories except for school-going listeners and not many of those. After mid morning, late evening is the time most favoured by radio presenters for short stories.

Everything I've said about making your work personal and immediate is twice as important here. It is a good medium for writing in the first person. The drawbacks of this method in novel-writing are well-known: with only one viewpoint, you can have only one storyline. Changes of scene and time must be clearly shown, preferably in dialogue. Make the most of this medium, as it favours the storyteller above the straight narrator.

Writers are seldom asked to read their own stories on

radio. This is normally done by an actor, more versed in the art than the writer is likely to be. Don't make it hard for the reader and confusing for listeners by including a lot of characters. If more than two are talking, make sure that their voices aren't too alike and that they don't use similar tricks of speech. Three speakers is plenty. The actor reading it will welcome the chance to dramatize the material and adopt the speech of the characters. He or she will cope with different accents and types of voice when reading dialogue, so that the read conversations are almost like a radio play. Don't make it hard for them by bringing a grumpy man's voice into dialogue between two women. You can avoid a sudden contrast by using a type of reported speech. It would be a female reader for a story aimed at female listeners.

' "Aren't you ever going to put that paper away?" asked Jill. Jack hunched his shoulders and rustled the pages noisily. He muttered that he hadn't read the sports section yet.'

In my story, 'Day Trip to Scarborough', the voices were those of a starchy elderly woman and a streetwise teenage girl from Leeds. There was no male voice, although there were male characters.

You must remember when writing for radio that the listener can't turn back the page as a reminder of what has gone before. Avoid subplots and names that appear only at the beginning and the end. Not everyone listens to a radio story sitting down and concentrating. They are just as likely to be driving in traffic or preparing a meal. This doesn't mean that you should simplify, just that you should avoid confusion.

8. NARRATIVE AND CONSTRUCTION

Stories are seldom used on local radio, although you can always enquire, but if you are local, you might easily get a prize-winning competition entry accepted and more than likely, the opportunity to read it yourself. Don't expect payment.

Your first novel just might be read on radio. Mine was, but people seemed to think at the time that there had to be an unflattering reason. 'I suppose you *know* somebody in BBC,' they said. My memoir, *Breakfast the Night Before*, has been read twice on RTÉ. Having done some research, I'm sure that a memoir or biography is much more likely to appear on radio. I will return to this later on.

Narrative

Show, don't tell. This has been the favourite maxim of writing tutors for at least thirty years. It is a reaction to the old-fashioned novel, which narrated the entire book from the outside, with the exception of dialogue.

Well yes, I go along with 'show, don't tell' most of the time, but I believe you need something in your narrative that isn't channelled through your characters' eyes and minds. I hardly ever leave that format, but there are times when you need to skew the writing in order to stay with it. You can tell rather than show when it's necessary without assuming a godlike position. You are writing a book, yes, but that entails telling a story.

Say you want to describe a room. It is huge, gloomy, painted in muddy colours, draped with threadbare hangings and the only person present is Cedric.

'Get Cedric to describe it, then,' you say.

'Ah, but Cedric is dead. A .5mm bullet from a .357 Magnum revolver ripped through his cold heart.'

'Oh. Well, Phoebe can see it when she arrives and notices the vast emperor-size bed with its –'

'Hang on. Phoebe and Cedric are – were – lovers. They were making mad passionate love in a hayfield the last time we met them. She's not going to notice the décor, she's going to rush blindly to Cedric's side in a storm of weeping.'

'It's not that kind of book.'

'All right, she's going to force herself to move towards the bed. Fighting back the tears ... she still wouldn't be concerned with the decorations. Neither would Cedric as he crawled dying towards the four-poster where, scant hours earlier ...'

A bit extreme maybe, but you don't *have* to filter everything through a character. If it's done so that it shows, you are overdoing it. Properly done you don't notice it, except to think how visual the writing is.

For decades, fine writers narrated every word except for dialogue. 'Showing' rather than 'telling' was achieved by the involvement of the characters.

For a novel that 'shows', first-person narration is ideal in a lot of ways, but not all. Tie yourself to one character and you tie yourself almost physically to him or her. In a crime novel, it is a favourite ploy, used successfully by Dick Francis, Sue Grafton, Robert Crais and many others. It is comforting, of course, to know that the narrator will magically dodge every attempt to kill him. There are drawbacks, however, especially in the antics

8. NARRATIVE AND CONSTRUCTION

necessary if the protagonist is going to be party to every turn of the plot. If you can pull it off, the method almost always results in a readable narrative, with pace and colour and that goes for a lot. A moderately interesting narrative told in the first person develops a certain style in almost every case.

In a novel, you need to vary the pace, but a popular thriller may tear along without slackening speed from beginning to end. Such a novel is often written in the first person and it is read as breathlessly as it is written, often at a sitting. It could be a wonderful read, tightly plotted and with an original twist and a shock ending. In a straight novel, breakneck speed isn't advisable.

The present tense is another popular style as, by its nature, it brings immediacy to the narrative. It's not as easy as it looks, though, because there are plenty of times when you have to revert to the past, to show what has gone before. If you mix your tenses, be sure to do it consistently.

In the novel I've been using for comparison, I fancied a first-person narrative for my protagonist, Ben, and even wrote a first chapter like that. When I read it back, I noticed that almost every line was intensely visual. I wondered how he would narrate after losing his sight. The answer was that he wouldn't. I left the first chapter as it stood and switched to the third person in the next.

> From the T-junction where you turn off, you can see the whole place … the grey two-storied house with the copper beeches in front of it, the new milking parlour, the fields with cows and sheep grazing in them.

PART ONE: FICTION

... When Grandmother's in a room, you don't notice the other people much. It's not just the funny clothes she wears, there's something about her. She stands out like a pheasant in a hen run.

Later on, when Ben was blind and just beginning to come to terms with it, I gave a 'Ben's eye view' of a journey through the countryside.

Ben listened to the traffic, automatically gauging its speed, weight and direction. His nose registered diesel oil, plastic, boot polish, tweed, tobacco and his own smell. There were dozens of distant smells too. Straw – somebody was combining, petrol, tar, grass ... it occurred to him that half the things he could hear or smell were invisible anyway.

Ben is a young man with little education, but plenty of imagination.

Straight narrative will bridge a gap, but don't go off into long descriptive passages, even if you do them well. It's a bit like dialogue: it must serve a purpose. Especially that of moving the story along.

'But what about plot?' you ask, reasonably enough. 'What's the use of telling us how to write and not telling us what to write about?' I think we need a new chapter for that.

9. What Readers Want and What You Can Give Them

Sex and violence

They want sex and violence. They always have and they always will. I repeated this at a workshop, where several people insisted that 'sex and violence' was a new and unpleasant development in fiction. I mentioned Shakespeare. 'Oh him,' they said.

Parson's daughter Emily Brontë didn't do badly either, nor did Thomas Hardy.

Of course, for raw sex and stomach-churning violence, you must turn to the Bible. Salomé's famous striptease was rewarded by the cold-blooded murder of the saint, John the Baptist. Then there is the story of Judith. Remember Judith, the great heroine? All the Judys we know are named after her.

PART ONE: FICTION

When King Holofernes' armies became a serious threat to the forces of Israel, Judith went to the king's tent at night and seduced him. Already drunk, she encouraged him to drink more until he fell into a deep sleep. Then she took his sword and hacked off his head. She took his head away with her as proof of her courage and resourcefulness.

The Bible stories still retain some shock value to anyone not brought up on them, mainly because they deal with shocking fact told simply. In a later age, Anne Frank's diary had more power to shock than many an award-winning novel of the Holocaust. Of course, fact is, or should be, more shocking than fiction.

I'm stressing this because there are plenty of people who tell me they'd love to write, but don't fancy all the sex and violence they think are required. If these activities are not your preferred subjects, you must woo your readers with something else, wonderfully plotted, convincingly peopled with fascinating characters and so gripping that they will read on when they are supposed to be doing something else – such as sleeping. But you won't get away from it. Sex and violence.

'Sex and violence' are teamed together in a phrase like 'eggs and bacon' or 'Laurel and Hardy'. But they have more in common than either of these; they combine to keep the human race going. Together they imply survival.

Deep down we are still primitive. Deep down what matters most to us is survival. It is of overwhelming interest to us. We must survive, so we must reproduce. In the Stone Age, your macho hero, having clubbed an antelope, would seek

9. WHAT READERS WANT AND WHAT YOU CAN GIVE THEM

out a likely woman, fight and kill her man and drag her to his cave where he would mate with her. Far from running away screaming rape, she would remain to share a romantic meal of raw antelope. The woman would stay with her mate, as the higher apes normally do, until he lost his looks (if any) and sex drive. Then a younger replacement would fight and probably kill him. As older women were less likely to be murdered than men, society was dominated by females, as gorilla society still is.

This isn't as far from *Woman's Own* as you might imagine. By the mid-twentieth century we had become adept at dressing up our primitive thoughts and actions in layer upon layer of verbiage. Consider the older-style women's magazines. The fiction concerns love and/or sex. The articles are about homes, fashion, cookery and babies. Shelter, warmth, food and reproduction. That is to say, survival.

The survivor always has been, always will be the most admired protagonist. The editors of *Reader's Digest*, once with the biggest fiction readership in the world, know this. All of their features and most of their fiction concerns survival. It isn't highbrow fiction, so plot wins out over literary merit, but character is most important.

In the straight survival story, the gallant hero or feisty heroine may easily end up dead, the stories being taken from life, but not until they have been through appalling ordeals. In fiction it's better if they stay alive. The writer becomes cynical and greedy after a time, and wants to leave a loose end or two to allow for a sequel.

PART ONE: FICTION

A small child who likes the same bedtime story over and over, might grow up to enjoy Mills & Boon romances, cheap thrillers, Westerns or any other kind of genre fiction. They are in effect reading the same bedtime story over and over with variations. The publishers of these books often issue a tip sheet to would-be authors, telling them how dress up the basic story.

Romances, in particular, embody simple storytelling with enough excitement to keep the reader turning the pages. In the charity bookshop that I supervise, it's noticeable that the most thumbed and faded copies are almost always Mills & Boon or Westerns, all written to a formula. There's something wholesome and comforting about a formula, even for an adult.

Romance writing is lucrative too. Charlotte Lamb, who also writes under at least five pseudonyms, produces a steady 15,000 words a day, without any revision. This would be more than one novel a week. She claims that anyone interested could write a book in less than twenty-eight days. Why am I expending so much time and energy, I ask myself? I haven't read her books, so am perhaps not entitled to judge, but I'm fairly sure that even the most basic romance should be written from the heart. I don't know how they can touch other hearts if they are dashed off to a set of rules. I've heard of a publisher that turns down dozens of such books because they have been written tongue in cheek, possibly by a serious writer seeking rapid cash. I've been told that I should just read blogs on the subject.

9. WHAT READERS WANT AND WHAT YOU CAN GIVE THEM

Back to plot or storyline. I keep avoiding this difficult aspect of writing fiction, although it is at the heart of the subject.

Conflict

The word occurs again and again in writing courses. You must have it. I sometimes think 'challenge' would be a more suitable word. The general idea is that you take a couple of characters, give them an aim, ambition or burning purpose, and block it. It might be blocked by another character or an event or series of events. Sooner or later, your key character overcomes the barrier and all ends happily.

This is over-simplification, but often the structure of a novel is just this. That person may have a number of barriers in his or her path and each one nastier than the last until the 'black moment' is reached, then Bingo! Success! Book finished.

The two principal plots, from which thousands of satellite plots are derived, are the seemingly insuperable difficulty or the agonizing choice. Don't despair, however. In the hands of a good writer, those simple plots are buried deep in the very guts of the book, unnoticed as a rule.

Plotting entails notes, a synopsis and a chapter by chapter breakdown if you are methodical and determined to work out a series of events and stick firmly to the blueprint. It's much better to be adaptable, to keep your imagination going, to be prepared to make changes, to eliminate a character that somehow doesn't fit in, to add or remove scenes as you go. I'm certain that, to be an original and able writer of fiction, you

PART ONE: FICTION

must be flexible. Be ready to rewrite, to re-imagine, just as your opinion of someone else's book may change as you read.

Some kind of synopsis is essential, to keep you on course and to remind you of ideas you may have forgotten, but don't be ruled by it. It's a memo to guide you rather than a corset for your imagination.

Crime

I've never written a crime book, I don't believe I could, but I read them all the time. A whodunit, in theory, should make an ideal subject for plot development. Often they do, but equally often they follow a set pattern. This type of book today is more slanted to character than in the past. This I think is because of the great detectives who have stamped their personalities on TV-watchers as well as readers. Colin Dexter's Inspector Morse is a good example.

The tough thriller, with a high body count and a tormented cop or private eye, who often seems as unlovable as his victims, is the norm at present. Some of these books are as well written as anything you are likely to read.

It's unfair that, in the book review pages of the newspapers, after the heading 'Books of the Week', with two or three reviews, there will be a sub-heading, 'Crime'. The best of these books have pared-down prose, at least two interesting characters and of course, lots of action. In addition there will be a consistent build-up of tension right up to the bloodbath a few pages from the end.

9. WHAT READERS WANT AND WHAT YOU CAN GIVE THEM

These are the books that I read in bed. No wonder I don't sleep well. As I write, it's Lee Child's latest, *Gone Tomorrow*. Told in the first person for a change, his laid-back wandering hero Jack Reacher is in an almost empty subway carriage at night, sitting opposite somebody he is convinced is a suicide bomber.

Child ratchets up the suspense by punctuating the scenes with the stopping and starting of the almost empty train.

> The train stopped at Astor Place. The doors hissed open. No one got on. No one got off. The doors thumped shut again and the motors whined and the train moved on …

The device had me fiercely withstanding the urge to skip to the next page. Resisting it, I read of Reacher's thoughts and the supposed bomber's body language for another fraught page and a half, then –

> The train stopped at Union Square. No one got on. No one got off. Hot air billowed in from the platform and fought the interior air conditioning. Then the doors closed again and the train moved on …

This tactic is used once more. If the phone had rung, I'd have let it ring. Lee Child is a master of the genre and he and a few other thriller writers are in no way inferior to most 'serious' writers. When Booker Prize-winner John Banville writes a thriller, he uses a pseudonym and keeps quiet, just as other superior writers do when they rename themselves and write romances.

PART ONE: FICTION

Writing for children

I have written two children's books, both of which were published by Poolbeg in Dublin. They did well and I believe one of them will be published in Irish, but I never felt tempted to specialize in them. I was starting a third when my editor left and I never went back because from what she said, I thought my stories would be wrong for her replacement.

Like so much of my work, *The Cow Watched the Battle* first appeared piecemeal in the *Tipperary Star*. The title story is not original, having been told to me at the age of ten or so. I used to ride my pony the mile and a half to Mrs Mackey's house. Tiny, white-haired, clad in layers of black, she would crouch on a low stool by the fire and tell stories. I remembered just two. Mrs Mackey would tell of the cow, lying on the hillside overlooking the Shannon, watching the invading Danes advancing up the mountain and the Irish rushing down to attack them. The story was rounded off by the milking of the cow, done morning and evening, exactly as usual.

Mrs Mackey sometimes lapsed into Irish when she reached the most exciting bits and I asked for the story every time I saw her. I wrote it as well as I could remember forty years later and it has been published on its own and anthologized.

The other story I used was called 'Manna from Heaven' and was set during the Famine. The people in Poolbeg wanted a dozen stories, for the six–ten age group and I used others, half-remembered, and invented a few more. I have read them aloud in schools often and children seem to enjoy them.

9. WHAT READERS WANT AND WHAT YOU CAN GIVE THEM

My second children's book, *The Other Side of the Island*, was a children's novel, aimed at girls from ten to twelve years old. This book was peppered with stories too. The letters I got from children, and they were many, gave me great insight into what they liked.

Supervising and stocking a second-hand bookshop is an ideal way to learn what appeals to different age groups. There aren't many parents buying books for their children without any idea of what they would like. On Saturdays the shop is full of children choosing their favourite authors and titles, some of them very young. They are choosey too and we keep a wish list for several.

Writing for children has been revolutionized in the last few years, first by J.K. Rowling and *Harry Potter*, then by Lemony Snicket, Darren Shan and Antony Horowitz, more recently Jacqueline Wilson and Stephenie Meyer.

Children wait for them and put down their names for the latest. The younger readers want *Horrid Henry* and pony books. More children are reading and they choose their own books and often like to discuss them.

I know from experience that a children's book must be pitched at a fairly narrow age group. I know too that however much your own children loved the stories you wrote for them, even children's book are part of the publishing industry, ruled by demand and difficult to second-guess. Publishers have their own ideas about illustrations too, so don't commission them unless you know they will be used.

PART ONE: FICTION

Nomenclature

I find I need names for my principal characters before I can write even the sketchiest synopsis. Sometimes I change a name because the one I've chosen is wrong and it niggles at me.

I like to have a name for the book as well, and fought for *Breakfast the Night Before* for my first memoir. This was what you had to have when going to Spancilhill Fair, which starts at first light on Midsummer's Day. The pundits at André Deutsch in London, who first published the book, wanted to change the title to *Tipperary Woman*, which appalled me. I'm glad I got my way there.

Location

Where do you plan to place your book, or at least the greater part of it? There's a horrid little tag we've all heard, 'Write about what you know.' It's not such good advice as it sounds. Depends what you know, of course.

I've lived on the edge of a town for almost ten years, but am still a countrywoman at heart, having spent all my life on a farm until the Millennium. What did I know when I started my first novel? A lot about horses and dealing in them, a fair amount about cattle and sheep, a lot about sheepdogs and sheepdog trials ... riveting stuff! Perhaps that's why few working farmers are novelists. It's certainly a reason for not even considering giving more than a couple of hours a day to writing.

In the past, there were two distinct types of 'country book'. One was the 'Big House' novel, depicting the lives of

9. WHAT READERS WANT AND WHAT YOU CAN GIVE THEM

the English upper classes, with tea on the terrace, a butler, two Labradors and possibly a corpse in the library. These were the forerunners of Jilly Cooper's rural blockbusters. I believe the huge popularity of these books is due almost as much to their settings as to their content.

The other type of country novel was first exemplified by Emily Brontë in *Wuthering Heights* and later by Mary Webb, whose books, especially *Precious Bane*, were immensely popular in the 1920s and 30s. Here you have a peasantry living in a perpetual state of high emotion, speaking a strange Gothic language: morbid, passionate and naïve. Mary Webb's style was hilariously parodied by Stella Gibbons in *Cold Comfort Farm*.

A less extreme form of this genre was found in Thomas Hardy's Wessex novels. Some have remained classics for more than a century. Hardy's novels didn't lack passion – some were faulted for immorality – but his rustic characters behaved believably, not like an alien race.

Some authors seemed to believe that emotions were nearer the surface in the country, that there was a thinner layer of social convention and hypocrisy. 'Rustics' were children of nature, torn by forces beyond their control. Therefore they chose a rural background for the nearest permitted approach to a 'steamy scene' and the phrase 'of the earth earthy' was coined. This idea was not correct. Country people were, and still are, more conventional than their city counterparts. But writing about a rural background offers fewer restrictions and a good setting for romance – provided it doesn't rain and you are not seeking to emulate D.H. Lawrence.

PART ONE: FICTION

Today's novels are mostly set in urban surroundings, real or imaginary. Reading reviews of new books, I notice how Irish authors stick to Irish cities, English ones to London, Oxford, Edinburgh and a few other familiar places. Most of the rest are in exotic locations abroad.

When I wrote *No Harp Like My Own*, I was accused of copying James Herriott. I was astonished. 'It's set in Yorkshire. You use Yorkshire dialect,' said my accuser. This shows up the shortage of country books. Herriott doesn't have a monopoly of Yorkshire.

It's hard to write a book with a farming background if you haven't one yourself. Research. And get someone better informed to check your work for bloomers. I once read a book where a prize cow gave two gallons of milk a day … any old cow would produce twice that amount!

Writing *No Harp Like My Own* was easy, because I knew the farm routine backwards. However, I had a deadline and had to write much of it during lambing.

Normally, I avoided writing at that time, as my long hours left me drained; my imagination curled up, hibernating. On this occasion I had no choice.

I remember sitting at the kitchen table, in duffle coat and jumper, trousers over my nightie, socks and wellies. I'd made up the fire and was writing while I waited for a ewe to lamb. It was 2 am and I was in the middle of a highly emotional scene, central to the book. As typing had to be error-free, I was scribbling away on a pad.

'… she experienced a moment of bewilderment …' or

9. WHAT READERS WANT AND WHAT YOU CAN GIVE THEM

would anxiety be better? Or even 'dread', perhaps? Leave a query in the margin, 'She wanted desperately to say …'

'Maa! Maa!' The summons was more compelling than anything Lesley might have said. Cursing, I went out into the night. The ewe looked smug. She seemed to be no nearer lambing than when I'd last checked on her. Back to the kitchen.

'… she experienced a moment of …' What? Hell, I'd forgotten. The thread was broken, my true-to-life characters reverted to cardboard. I turned back and reread the chapter, trying to keep my eyes open. But the chapter began in a lambing shed, with Ben deftly delivering a lamb. It had seemed like a good idea at the time … an hour later I went to have a look at the ewe and found her peacefully suckling twins. But another ewe was starting.

Back in the kitchen, the words danced before my eyes and the clock struck three. Then suddenly from my unconscious mind came a flow of words. I wrote without pause to the end of the chapter and, vitality regained, rushed to the shed and delivered another lamb. Then I went briskly up to bed.

The chapter was certainly the best in the book and I have used it on its own for readings. It was written with an immediacy that I couldn't sustain and is a slice of life as solid as a slice of cake.

There must be a lesson here and, while I don't recommend going to such extreme lengths for true authenticity, it's no harm to be directly involved with your subject.

A townsperson has one advantage when writing about the country: the gift of freshness. Those of us who were born and brought up in the country sometimes become immune to its charms, especially if we have to work out of doors in all weathers. We hardly notice the beauty of our surroundings; we grumble about isolation and small earnings.

When I lived in a beautiful wooded area, close to a lake, I spent my holidays in cities. When I tried to set the scene on an Irish farm, I had to look on it with the eyes of a stranger. I found it much easier to describe rural Yorkshire, which I first visited in my late twenties. Familiarity breeds not contempt so much as acceptance.

You shouldn't be in a rush to set your novel in the Caribbean or the Himalayas. Research is expensive and not always effective. You may have a more suitable location on your doorstep. Learn to observe your surroundings as if you were a tourist, seeing them for the first time. Describe country scenes as if you spent your working hours in a windowless office and your evenings in a poky apartment. The town dweller is probably blind to its architecture and the charm of its byways. When, after first visiting Leeds, I mentioned its charm, I was greeted with loud laughter by people who lived there. Yet Leeds *is* charming, once you get away from its soulless centre. It took a stranger's eye to notice it.

This brings me to a difficult point. Most country people are different. Neither better nor worse: different. The nearest urban equivalent to a small farmer is a small shopkeeper and these get fewer as the global giants buy them up. The shopkeeper is at the mercy of recession, inflation, break-ins and other man-made disasters, but isn't greatly affected by the

9. WHAT READERS WANT AND WHAT YOU CAN GIVE THEM

weather. Farmers, no matter how efficient, are still slaves of the elements, as they have been since the earth was first tilled. Floods or drought can put a small farmer out of business; so can abnormal snowfall or prolonged frost. Storms can wreck their buildings, lightning kill their cattle.

These unavoidable risks mark a person's character. They aggravate pride and obstinacy and a certain fatalism. Much of what Thomas Hardy wrote is still true today and it would pay students of the genre to read *Far from the Madding Crowd*.

The pace of country life is slow, but it is life that is slow, not the people who live it. Farmers may be industrious, energetic, always eager to finish a job and get on to the next. The inexorable routine of seedtime and harvest can frustrate such a character to a point where he or she is at best difficult to live with, at worst violent or even insane. A stable personality is needed in order to survive.

Getting fiction published is largely a matter of fashion and the Green movement is making the country fashionable. Children are learning about ecology and nature books are everywhere. These children who are being taught the value of clean air, space in which to breathe it and the rights of wild creatures, are tomorrow's readers. I believe there will be a demand for country books for many years to come.

My other novels have been historical, or at least 'period', so their location wasn't a matter of choice. If I were to choose an exotic location, I'd choose an imaginary one in a known area, such as a Spanish or Pacific island with an invented name. Readers might wonder where the book was set, but it would be a mixture of several places known to me. I have done this in a few short stories.

No matter where you set your book, you must have a feeling for place, as you have for the people who inhabit it.

Earlier I mentioned conflict, the state of being at odds with somebody or something. It doesn't have to be another person. A character could be in conflict with his career, his lover, with nature, with God or even with himself. He could also easily be at odds with his surroundings, especially if his way of life had been forced on him by circumstances beyond his control.

There are plenty of romances and love stories (no, these are not synonymous), where a countryman, slow in mind and speech, falls violently in love with a quick-witted young woman brought up in a busy town. In the romances, he suffers but adapts, in the love stories, she leaves him, but with regret.

I wrote a long short story, showing the reverse: quick-witted young man from the city falls in love with agricultural young woman, unwilling or unable to compromise. Fearing that it might be mistaken for a glimpse into my own life, I left it in a drawer.

10. Starting to Write a Novel

Openings

Let us imagine that you have thought up some interesting characters, placed them in positions where straight ahead isn't an option (it seldom is), and the lives of your two or three key characters are at a crossroads. You have known these people for some time now, where they live, why they behave as they do, their names, their looks. It should now be possible to weave a plot round them.

Your first page is important, not just because of your future readers, but also because agents, editors, publishers and reviewers, while they may not read every word, will certainly read the first page of your submission with attention. Never drift into a book, give it a memorable beginning and a well-written first paragraph.

PART ONE: FICTION

Again, we can sometimes learn from the works of thriller writers, who know how easily their readers can be put off by a slow start.

Later in this chapter, you will find a list of what I consider to be words and catchphrases that I don't think should ever be used in fiction. In the mouths of characters they will pass, but not in narrative. Here, for example, you will find 'upmarket' and 'downmarket'. They are useful words that mean something, but certainly don't add to the beauty of your writing. I will now use one of them. Openings in upmarket fiction, literary award winners and the like, may be quirky or downright peculiar, but they should have a quality, a flavour, which compels the reader to continue.

Some writers throw away the potential of a beginning that should hook the reader, by walking into the narrative. You can, or should be able to, write a noteworthy opening, which links up with the story later on, if necessary. Some celebrated writers can make anything noteworthy, with no apparent effort.

Recently I read *The Secret Scripture* by Sebastian Barry and *The English Patient* by Michael Ondaatje, both award-winning, both grim in a number of ways. I read Barry because I had to review it. The first two lines, which tell that what follows is an ancient woman's diary written in a mental asylum, put me off. Then I thought, oh hell, I'll have to read it, and tried the first paragraph of narrative. After that I was hooked by the beauty and *difference* of the words. A description of a river in Sligo, carrying rubbish to the sea, doesn't sound promising. Read it, if you haven't already, and you will see what I mean.

I avoided reading *The English Patient* for some time, because I had heard only of grisly bits like the hacking off of someone's thumbs. When I finally read it, I discovered that the thumbs were removed off screen so to speak and it is a powerful and lovely book. The opening paragraph is beautifully expressed, so that you want to read on; the second and third introduce a mystery. I'm sorry that I let Caravaggio's thumbs put me off for so long.

Denis Lehane's *Mystic River* is a novel with a quirky beginning, in this case a literary device that worked: 'It was the afternoon of my eighty-first birthday and I was in bed with my catamite when Ali announced that the archbishop had come to see me.' (This has been quoted as an example by someone else, but I can't remember who it was.)

Endings

Endings depend so much on what has gone before that I can hardly lay down rules. The popular genres go in for happy endings, but these have changed. A generation back, 'happy' meant married (in white) to the desired partner, or riding into the sunset, again with that special person. Now endings are more temporary, a more permanent arrangement with one's boyfriend, bloke, fella, significant other, fiancé or main squeeze. Whatever the outcome, it's positive. I've checked out some samples of 'bloke lit', or 'lad lit', and the endings were not permanent, more likely to be a party or a booze-up, with a promise of more to follow.

Away from purely commercial fiction, there is a much wider choice. Some writers seem to go out of their way to prevent their protagonists ending up happier than they started. I think that unless it's true and tragic, a book should end on a high note: a memory, a question, the hope for a sequel.

I once judged a story competition in which the story I liked best was ruined by the sudden death at the very end of the key character. Afterwards I asked the author why she had killed the character. 'You have to avoid a happy ending,' she said.

There's a difference between a sense of positive closure and happy ever after, tied up with pink ribbons. Killing off a character whom readers have learned to like *for no obvious reason*, is gratuitous, just as sex and violence are gratuitous when they seem to have been added in order to pump up the drama. Or the sales.

Learning from others

You should never stop reading: fiction for choice if that's what you are writing. Learn to edit in your head as you read. Imagine you are editing your own work. Be critical and intelligent and whenever you think, 'That's not right,' ask yourself why it isn't. I've been editing for writers for several years and have learned a lot myself from the experience. If you are enjoying the book you are reading, ask yourself, why? If not, again, why?

10. STARTING TO WRITE A NOVEL

Go over your work and edit it from time to time. Whenever I return to my current book, I turn back to where I started the last section and go through it carefully. If this isn't you, don't worry. Some writers do a whole draft without a backward glance, others polish obsessively as they go. Find out what suits you best, but do cultivate your critical faculties at all times.

Research

Again, as you read other authors' books, read observantly, you may learn some useful things. When you need to research as you write, the Internet may help, or it may not. Check your sources ... and don't get sidetracked and still be googling away hours later. Research is addictive at times.

My third novel, *Renegade,* concerned a character from two hundred years ago, who had never been researched. It took me a couple of years to unearth enough about him to write the book. I learned that newspaper archives are the very devil. I went to the National Library in Dublin every week and studied microfiches, which left me with a blinding headache and little else. (Someone stole my handbag while I was there, complete with money and train ticket. I had to go to the *Irish Times* offices and borrow a tenner from Kevin Myers.) I searched records and got in a muddle. My most valuable lesson learned was never to flounder. It wastes time. I would advise anyone faced with serious and necessary research to ask an expert.

PART ONE: FICTION

Later, still without some badly needed material on the Prittie family of my novel, I asked about Archives when in the National Library. 'They're next door, upstairs,' said the man I asked. It took me a while to find somebody with the time and inclination to let me in. 'We haven't quite finished organizing the material,' he said.

He was right. We climbed several flights of stairs in the august Georgian building, arriving in a large room full of overflowing cardboard boxes. 'I think the Prittie stuff is over by the window,' said my guide. He then left me to do my own research.

It was slow, but it was fascinating. I'd say the boxes were sent to Dublin when Kilboy House was partly demolished and rebuilt in the Fifties. Desks and cupboards must have been emptied of everything, letters and files pulled out in armfuls and dumped into boxes. I recognized my mother's handwriting on an envelope and found a reply to an invitation to play bridge in 1933.

I had asked the Arts Council for a research grant, or any sort of grant. I was neglecting my farm. They wrote back saying that if I had a farm I could sell a field. They must have thought that fields were cheap or that my expected advance was going to be princely.

By the time the book came out, I'd got a computer and thought I'd check on the validity of my research. There was quite a lot, all agreeing with the material I'd used, so I was delighted. Then I noticed that the material had been researched by Marjorie Quarton …

10. STARTING TO WRITE A NOVEL

The power of language

Kipling said, 'Words are the most powerful drug used by mankind.' Spoken words are certainly a powerful drug, provided they are spoken by a charismatic person, sure that he's right. Hitler, Churchill, Martin Luther King. People who could find the right words and use them with absolute conviction have swayed thousands, and since radio and television, millions.

The written word is hardly as powerful, but literature is sprinkled with quotes that are famous and go on being famous down the years. Words are beautiful things that anyone can play with, twisting and turning them to convey nuances of meaning, to astonish, to move, even to frighten. In case you hadn't noticed, I love them. I like to find out where they came from, what language was their source and what the original meaning. The poet Milton had such a dislike of Germanic and Anglo-Saxon words that every one he used in *Paradise Lost* is from the Greek or Latin.

Our language, though, is also full of meaningless, colourless and above all useless words, and you just can't get away from them. Here is a list of pet hates.

Note: If this is how a character in your book speaks, the rules don't apply. He or she may be a politician.

Aka This is an abbreviation of 'also known as'. Nasty little word. We did very nicely without it.

PART ONE: FICTION

Moniker Or any other bit of Cockney used for comic effect by non-Cockneys

Boasted (for had, or featured) The house boasts fourteen bedrooms, all en suite. Leave it to the estate agents.

Cough up (as spend) Dated slang. Fine for Wodehouse and for boys' books of an earlier age.

Garner It means a granary, or in past times, to gather grain. Why garner information?

Paucity A paucity of members, or ideas, or food. An ugly word, while 'scarcity' is perfectly harmless, quite pleasant in fact.

Pen (as a verb) Old-world romantic Elizabeth Barrett Browning penned her sonnets, I'm sure. 'Penning' a novel or article sounds pretentious and silly.

Funky Originally used for jazz. Now it could be just about anything. Hope it soon dies.

Eatery Don't know why this one makes me cringe.

Chortled, chuckled, joked, opined and quipped Used as alternatives for 'said'. Discussed earlier.

Went As an alternative for said. As in, '… then she turned round and went "How dare you!!!"'

10. STARTING TO WRITE A NOVEL

Tome Book, please.

Hopefully Not as popular as it was. Or perhaps it's used so much that I've stopped hearing it.

Thankfully As above. There are several more in the same vein.

Absolutely This is a habit. I do it myself. It means nothing as we use it.

Actually (usually pronounced 'Ackshly') Favourite word of people being interviewed on radio. May occur a dozen times in succession, qualifying every statement. 'Actually it was raining, but I hadn't actually brought an umbrella, so actually we both got wet.'

Obviously ('Oviously') I've written about flowing words. This one can't flow and brings a corner into every sentence, with its central 'bvi'. Popular with beginner writers, who use it unwisely. 'She was wearing what was obviously a new dress.' If it was obvious, why mention it? She was wearing a new dress.

Infrastructure Another nasty word with corners. Don't say it if you have had a drink or two and never if you wear ill-fitting false teeth.

Probably ('Probly' or even 'Prolly'). Another one for the interviewee. (Ow! That's another hate …) It's a harmless enough word written down.

PART ONE: FICTION

Meaningfulness and *Meaninglessness*. Don't need to say anything about these pests.

Basically ' "Basically, I'm a woman," started the bright young female interviewee.' 'Basically' permeates everything. I checked and discovered it can mean 'merely', 'practically' and 'principally'. It is also used as a word to finish off a sentence. 'So I went to college and returned after getting my degree. Basically.' Hope it wasn't a degree in English.

Promptly Another non-flowing word. Beginners use it for comic effect. It doesn't work. 'He turned green and promptly threw up on the carpet.' Not funny anyway, but 'promptly' doesn't help at all.

Scenario/Worst-case scenario Recent clichés, here to stay, I'm afraid. A pleasing word written down and looks as if it ought to mean something. Ah. It means a master plan. I've checked.

Diaspora Made popular by Mary Robinson. People often use it without knowing what it means. Originally it referred to the Jews when they were dispersed among the Gentiles. Now it means a group of people who have been dispersed, but it's often used as if it was a place.

Upmarket/Downmarket Useful workhorse words. I don't like them in narrative. See above. There are dozens of new portmanteau words in the dictionaries of today.

10. STARTING TO WRITE A NOVEL

Arguably 'Debatable' is the nearest I can get to a synonym.

I could go on. The read-aloud test, which I have been suggesting at intervals, should help to weed out the worst offenders.

Fashion

This is something I've touched on, as you must avoid dated slang and dated behaviour unless you are writing a period novel. If you are of course, you must research these things carefully.

I must revert to the business of writing short stories for women's magazines for a minute, because these are more severely bound by fashion than full-length books written for a similar readership. Read some of them to get the idea. Is good always rewarded and evil always punished? Bear it in mind. If you aren't sure what age group the journal caters for, check the advertisements. Are they for dating agencies and Club Med holidays? Stairlifts and Zimmerframes? Couldn't be easier, could it?

As for novels, I can only repeat, keep reading them and read reviews and publishers' magazines, because soon you will be approaching those publishers and, although you can only guess what they are going to want, it's easy to discover what they don't want.

Most of them get unsolicited offerings of material, which is totally unsuitable.

In conclusion

When you have finished writing your novel, I suggest you let it rest quietly in a drawer or on a disk. Let it incubate for a few weeks. Then look through it. As a part-time writer, you have been neglecting all kinds of things since the end appeared within your sights. Ideas for revision, second thoughts about scenes, sudden realization that you have been borrowing from a favourite author, will drop into your mind when least expected.

Allow yourself at least one full day to deal with it, possibly two or three. You've written in dribs and drabs, so as to nurture a hobby ... which might develop into a career. Drip-feeding your work isn't ideal, but if you are wholehearted, you'll have made it succeed for you. The fallow time when it rests in that drawer is important. Imagine that someone else has written the book and has asked you to look through it and suggest ways of improving it. I have found this method the best way of being impartial and far better than making excuses for yourself, as you will if you can't dream up better alternatives where they are needed ...

It is possible to 'write a book to death', I've seen it done. One or two people whose books I edited just couldn't agree that their work was as good as it was ever going to be. They wrote and rewrote, cutting, inserting; improving some things but writing the freshness out of others. This isn't as hard to do as you might expect. Don't be hard on yourself, be fair with yourself.

Some authors talk about all the drafts they write and this

10. STARTING TO WRITE A NOVEL

used to fill me with horror. Setting down all those thousands of words once would be slave labour if you were being paid by the hour. But three or four times? Forget it.

11. Getting down to Business

The finished book

Now for the boring stuff. Read your original synopsis, or whatever breakdown you used when writing, and use it as a basis for the one you will certainly need. Probably you will find that the book has deviated from the original outline in a big way. So rewrite the synopsis in line with the finished book. Most publishers ask for such a short outline that it's hard to do justice to a novel of normal length, so pick out the bare bones of the narrative. When you have done this, count your words and, if you have some to spare in order to reach the stingy minimum, use them wisely.

There is a sneaky way around this wish for few words. Instead of merely sending a covering letter and the stunted synopsis, add a page entitled, 'Submission', or 'Proposal'. This is exactly what it says. It doesn't deal with characters or plot,

II. GETTING DOWN TO BUSINESS

but does describe the genre and the central theme of your work. I believe (my publisher may not agree) that most sheets of paper with just a dozen lines of typescript on them, get read. So put it in with the synopsis, covering letter and whatever part of your book you are hoping to impress with.

Presentation

It is difficult to get a first novel accepted. You already know that. So make your attempt in a spirit of cheerful hopefulness if you can, but let it be tempered with some of that dreary commodity, common sense. Make your proposal look as attractive as possible. There's something inviting about a block of paper topped with a nicely spaced and judged title page. Even an e-mail attachment should be made to look as interesting as possible, but don't mess about with fancy script or borders.

You can learn about presentation anywhere, but just remember that this varies from one country to another and go for advice that caters for your own. Publishers' ideas are different in the USA, for example. I've had a book published there in hardback and was sent a list of dos and don'ts that surprised me.

When you send away a manuscript, don't forget to put a title page on top and whatever you do, don't skimp on materials. Don't use cut-price copying paper, give plenty of space to your paragraphs, allow good margins and adequate room for chapter headings. It used to be the norm to double-space, but

PART ONE: FICTION

now that the computer has revolutionized editing, I find that most people are happy with 'one and a half' spacing.

You can paper-clip chapters together if you like, but most of the publishers I've dealt with like the whole manuscript loose. This makes me nervous. Pack it into a box, such as the one that quality A4 paper comes in, having first wrapped it in plastic film. Post the box within a padded bag, with return postage (international, not stamps or, heaven help us, cash) and hope for the best. Oh, and do buy a new padded bag. I have received stuff to edit in much labelled and postmarked bags, oozing chopped-up grey mush at the corners.

When I started writing stories for a magazine, I discovered after a while that I was writing a book. This hadn't been my intention and I was delighted. The book eventually appeared entitled *One Dog and his Man* and twenty-five years later is still in print. Three publishers have brought it out and it has also appeared in French and in a handsome edition in Japanese.

Getting it into print was something else. To start with, it was – is, a funny book. 'Very, very funny,' said one of its reviewers, as did the modest fan club that I enjoyed. Funny books weren't wanted at the time, I was told. I didn't know what to do with it. Another black mark, apparently, was that it was an animal book and concerned Shep, who lived at Coolcoffin in County Galway. Animal books were not wanted either, said the people I told about it. My husband was convinced that anyone would be delighted to publish such a masterpiece, or else I think I'd have abandoned it.

11. GETTING DOWN TO BUSINESS

After dithering for months, I said, 'I'll send it to the first publisher I see.' Off I went to church and opened my prayerbook, which had been published by Collins in London. The next day, I packed my slender work, neatly handwritten in script as easy to read as print, and sent it off to Collins.

It was read. It was returned. The letter turned the book down and that was enough for me. Too short, they said. I should type it. They liked the illustrations and would love to see anything else I had to offer, they added. Good luck and do keep in touch.

It's strange to think, looking back, what a tiny amount I knew about getting books published, considering that I read addictively. Tiny amount? I didn't know anything.

I didn't understand that this was not a rejection, but encouragement from one of the most prestigious publishing houses in the world. Real rejections come on printed forms, signed by a secretary: 'not suitable for our list' is a favourite phrase.

I showed the book to the late Charles Chenevix Trench, a distant relative and a fine writer. His *History of Horsemanship* had recently appeared and he was signing my copy. Charles offered to introduce me to his agent, David Fletcher, an excellent and totally reliable man, based in Edinburgh, who took me on at once. I don't think he held out many hopes for *One Dog*, however, he sent the typed manuscript to eight publishers. Six turned it down and the other two lost it between them, each blaming the other. David gently advised me to consider another occupation but by then I was bitten, so to speak, with the writing bug. I asked him to try just one more publisher. He did and the Blackstaff Press in Belfast accepted it. Before it came out, they'd asked for a sequel and I had almost finished it.

So far I haven't been offering advice on finding an agent, but by the time you finish your book, you should have been putting out feelers for some time. Unless an agent or someone professionally involved in the publishing trade is known to you, it's a waste of time approaching one until you have your material complete and ready for its fate. I was lucky and David still deals with all my earlier books. I have looked after the more recent ones myself, those that were published in Ireland, since the arrival of the euro.

The reviews for my little book were fantastic and appeared in national papers. The launch was in Belfast and in 1984 Belfast wasn't a city to visit if you could avoid it. Another book came out at the same time; mine didn't have a launch to itself and I stayed at home and waited to see it in the shops. I waited in vain. Eason's didn't carry it and it was only sold in shops that had made a point of ordering it. The few shops that stocked it in the Republic placed it in any category they fancied, while would-be customers searched in all the others. It sold out in the North and was reprinted and followed by the sequel. And that was that for a while.

Blackstaff were good to deal with and allowed me to sell the book myself, but neither I nor my agent profited much at the time.

There are some points of interest here for the aspiring writer. Bookshops have to classify their books. Mine spanned several categories: Humour, Animal, Irish interest and Children, although it wasn't a children's book as such. Of the hundreds of letters I've got concerning it over the years, the vast majority are from adults, but the ages span from seven to eighty plus.

When it went out of print, Farming Press in England bought the rights and published the two books in one and it's still around with farming books and videos and is also to be had in large print and audio formats.

I've talked about this book at some length because from an unpromising start it led me to write for leading publishers and to be a moderate success. My part-time status kept me back a bit; there were occasions when I'd gladly have spent all my waking hours writing but couldn't. However, I don't regret my decisions.

Humorous fiction

Before I move on, a word about funny books. Humorous books. I hate the word 'humorous'. One provincial newspaper decided to give me a review and said that, 'Children might enjoy the book although the grammar wasn't always correct; but we think some of this must have been intended to be of a humorous nature.' That review went in the bin.

Think long and hard before starting to write anything of 'a humorous nature'. What makes one person fall about laughing doesn't raise a smile from someone else. Because many people thought my book was funny, I got a reputation for

PART ONE: FICTION

writing amusingly. Sometimes I do, but not by trying to. There is nothing less amusing than something written by an author determined to make his readers laugh, because the harder he tries, the less amusing he is. Not always, of course, but often enough. So if you want to amuse, don't try too hard. What is less funny than a nervous novice stand-up comedian? And the comedian has the advantage of directly speaking to his audience and can try to engage its sympathies when he flounders.

It's impossible to write humour that will appeal to an unlimited readership. Tom Sharpe's reputation as a comic writer is merited, but for everyone who laughs their way through his books there is another who is bored, indifferent or finds him distasteful.

Terry Pratchett gets his laughs by an original line in deadpan humour, based on fantastic situations and a strange medley of characters. His following is vast, but a percentage of readers don't find him even mildly amusing.

Humour in books is more valued than it was twenty years ago, when it was still regarded as a rather disreputable branch of 'real writing'. Cartoons have always been popular and *The Simpsons* is probably the most widely viewed and read humour today.

The chapter in this book entitled 'Dialogue' was originally thought up for a workshop I held many years ago. While most of the people there enjoyed it, one man said peevishly, 'Why must you always try to be funny?' This was below the belt and floored me completely. For once I was speechless. However, nearly everyone in the class had a comment to offer and he

II. GETTING DOWN TO BUSINESS

was routed. 'Because it's easier to remember something if it amuses you,' was the general response. About five years later, I edited a novel for somebody who had been present and she recalled the occasion, saying she'd never forgotten my silly little snippets of dialogue.

I'd like to quote a sample from the late Ivor Brown as an example of bathos or anti-climax. It's taken from *Something for Nothing* by H. Vernon Dickson.

'She threw herself about and into his arms and clung to him fiercely. "You're no good," she whispered, "but I'm crazy about you. I loathe and I – I guess I love you too. There's a word for it – ambivalence." To this display of erudition by the amorous lady, the terse and masculine answer was, "Yeah."'

So I read it and have remembered it ever since. I've listened to lectures and read instructions by the score and forgotten every word.

One Dog and his Man had been out a few weeks when I got a letter from Collins in London. They didn't know that the book had been accepted and wanted another look. I was amazed, but sent along a copy, with a couple of clippings.

Within a few days, I got a phone call from the commissioning editor, offering me the job of writing a novel about a dog mascot in World War II. I didn't know what to say, so asked for more information. They sent me photos, a couple of letters and some newspaper cuttings and I read them with disappointment. Having a first novel commissioned by such a notable house should have been a wonderful break for anyone, but I knew I couldn't do it.

PART ONE: FICTION

For a start, the dog belonged to an American unit and I knew less than nothing about the subject. I would have to invent American characters and I hardly knew any Americans. Then the dog, which looked appealing in a photograph, needed to be more than just appealing. He was a terrier, called Bob or maybe Bill. The men loved him and taught him tricks. He took part in the Victory Parade.

My husband was ill and died the following year, so I spent a lot of time sitting with him. Late at night I read books or tried to think of a way to make Bob – or Bill – into a war hero. It wasn't working. I knew I'd have to try to contact people who remembered the dog, while being acutely aware that their memories were more likely to be of the victory than the parade. *I can't do it. I can't turn it down. What on earth am I to do?*

Thinking like this, I decided to read for an hour and forget dog mascots and battles long ago. I went to a tall Georgian bookcase and reached up to the top shelf, so high that the books were seldom disturbed. As I levered one out, its neighbour crashed to the floor and fell face up, open at a photograph. If I put what followed in a novel, I'd be accused of stretching credulity, but it can't be helped. It happened.

The photograph was of Corporal Jack, regimental mascot of the 2nd Battalion, the Royal Dublin Fusiliers in World War I. I knew a lot about that, but had forgotten. The book fell open because, when I was very small, my father who served in the regiment right up to 1922 when it was disbanded, used to show me the picture and tell me the story. It always ended: '… and so Jack was decorated and promoted'. In the photograph, he wears his medals and wound stripes on his tunic.

I had a lot of papers and maps of my father's, because at one time he had been presumed dead and all his letters and belongings were sent back to his supposed widow. They eventually turned up at my home and I dived eagerly into the boxes of maps and battle orders.

Well, Collins fell in with my suggestion and the book, *Corporal Jack,* was born. As John died while I was writing it, the success it had was overshadowed and I was reluctant to join in publicity. I should have, of course. I paid for that by having hardly any publicity for my next book, but hearing *Corporal Jack* read on radio gave me a thrill.

It was lucky that I had an agent then, as the book went into all sorts of editions and was optioned by cable TV in America. Later, *No Harp Like My Own* was optioned by Touchstone, and Geena Davies was apparently keen to play the heroine. It never happened, of course, but the fees came in handy, especially as we were in the middle of a recession. David Fletcher was knowledgeable and capable. He checked my contracts and fought for subsidiary rights.

Finding an agent

When people ask me how to secure an agent, I can only advise them to look them up and contact the most promising. Be careful, though, not everyone follows this advice and you can waste time and money shopping around.

If you have friends in the writing or publishing business, you might persuade one of them to recommend you to an agent. Don't expect anyone to do this until they have seen your work and decided that it deserves to be read.

Yes, you can manage without an agent and yes, you would be better off without if the alternative is a bad agent, but beginners drowning in conflicting advice and not having literary connections should try for a good one. A good agent will probably get you a bigger advance and higher royalties than you could raise yourself. Think about it. Agents make a living out of percentages of 10 per cent, perhaps 12.5 per cent, occasionally as much as 15 per cent. If they don't get top rates of pay, those percentages won't keep them in business.

Good agents not only understand the publishing business, they have friends in it. Many started by working in publishing firms. They know what they can swing and what they can't.

First-time authors are often shy about selling themselves. Good agents aren't shy about anything. They may be nice people, lovely people, but their first concern is to sell both you and your book in order to earn a good living. They also negotiate rights, such as film and TV rights, and act as go-betweens in arguments. Most publishers like to work with an agent and a lot of them won't consider submissions that come without one, while others won't consider those that do.

The fact remains that agents are busy and scarce. Personally, I wouldn't want to be represented by a barely willing, overworked person, who was taking me on as a concession. Your agent should be enthusiastic about your book and want to work with you. Agents appear to have all the writers they

II. GETTING DOWN TO BUSINESS

need on their books and unless yours appeals to them on sight, you may well be turned down.

Before you offer your work, you may like to show it to a professional editor. This is difficult for me to write about, as I am a professional editor myself. Here I speak from my own experience. Editing may be 'copy', which takes care of spelling, grammar, typos and basic presentation. Or it may be 'substantive', also called 'concept' editing, which means that, in addition to the above, words and sentences are altered, sometimes rewritten, when the sense or style demand it.

A good editor will also tidy up the presentation and be prepared to talk with you or communicate, when explanations are needed.

This editor may well be the first person to read your book and if he or she is freelance as opposed to being paid by a publisher, may refuse to edit your book because, in his or her opinion, no amount of editing will make it publishable. Getting a book edited isn't cheap and it would be unprofessional to accept the job.

This is where rejection blues set in. Of course the person will be kind and will explain carefully why he or she would prefer not to take on the book. It's a hard one, this, because it's difficult to assess your own work in a balanced way, but you do need a second opinion before you proceed. You must learn to accept criticism without flying to bits, and then decide how fair it is. Keep cool and listen. You may suddenly be able to see your faults through someone else's eyes. You may be required to do considerable rewriting.

PART ONE: FICTION

This is when positive thinking is essential. It's possible to force yourself to write, but not to write well. You need to remember those criticisms, even though you are longing to forget them. Write your way back into the book and address everything you think you can improve.

Your agent will offer your book to publishers, but if you have contact with anyone in the publishing business, be careful to tell them about your agent.

If you have tried everything and still haven't got one, try checking your favourite books, published in your own country for choice, to see if the authors have acknowledged an agent. I've been told that this works by people who have tried it, but haven't first-hand experience.

So you haven't managed to secure a good agent? Try again when you've had a book published. It's easier then, I'm told.

Writers' and publishers' magazines have lists of them, as they generally name the agent representing the latest exciting new voice in fiction. Check them out. Go to workshops and anywhere that a published writer is a speaker and try to pick his or her brains about agents.

Still no luck? Then you must try doing without, which is sad, because if an established agent agrees to represent you, it's a sign that he or she thinks your book can or should be published and few agents are gamblers.

12. Going it Alone

Finding a publisher

Go to the nearest large bookshop and spend a lot of time there. Or try a library. You should have a mental list or, if forgetful, a written one, of books that you have really enjoyed during the past year or so.

Find the books and check who published them. You can do this a lot more easily and quickly online, so it's for you to choose. I'd use the computer, but then I usually do.

There aren't nearly as many publishers about as there were when *Corporal Jack* appeared. Publishing houses were folding or being taken over by bigger firms every day in the 1980s. Collins itself had a huge internal reshuffle. After taking two novels from me, they were willing to take another and I sent them *Renegade,* which they liked, but they turned down because the central character was a cleric. I couldn't

PART ONE: FICTION

change the profession of a historical protagonist, even had I wanted to, but I was in luck when André Deutsch accepted the book.

I had a happy time writing for André Deutsch. In the Eighties, being Irish was not a selling point. I was made to feel this when I was writing for Collins, although my editor, Margery Chapman, certainly never mentioned it. The firm was taken over by Rupert Murdoch and the Chapmans set up their own firm while I was with the company.

It's difficult for me to divide fiction from non-fiction (which has its own section in this book). But my move to Deutsch from Collins happened when Collins turned down my memoir, *Breakfast the Night Before*. David Fletcher then sent it to Deutsch, who accepted it and so I got to know part-owner and commissioning editor, Diana Athill.

Diana, herself a distinguished author, excelled herself in 2009, when she won the Costa Prize for non-fiction at the age of ninety-two, with her memoir, *Somewhere Towards the End*.

Diana had a coup when she accepted Molly Keane's *Good Behaviour*, which had been turned down by Methuens and she hoped for a second one. She personally loved my book and didn't alter anything except some dubious punctuation when she edited it.

She wanted a novel, so I took the partly written *Renegade* out of its drawer and sent it along. It was accepted and at the same time I had a request for a follow-up to *'Breakfast'*, which I called *Saturday's Child*.

12. GOING IT ALONE

I was writing both books at the same time and it was not the best of times, because Deutsch went bankrupt. The result for me was that I had to speed up the ending of *Saturday's Child*, but effects were more far-reaching. *Renegade* wasn't reviewed in Ireland, review copies and press releases didn't appear and I had to buy up as many books as I could afford and sell them myself. As I've said, Irish politics was not a favourite theme in England then, and sales were poor. It did better here, but I still had a cartload to sell myself. Ironically, now that the book is hard to find, it is in demand.

All this is to show that finding and acquiring a publisher doesn't guarantee success. My next novel fared even worse. Commissioned by Deutsch after Diana Athill had read the incomplete book, I'd written 120 pages and didn't have a signed contract when the firm went down. Mind you, it surfaced again almost at once, but too late for my book, which is called *The Keepsake*. Other British publishers turned it down, but I got an enquiry from the TV station that produced *Coronation Street*.

'Too Irish,' they said, 'set it in Britain.' I got the same response from two more publishers, so I began to transfer parts of the book to pre-World War II England. When this was almost done, I contacted a firm that had been moderately interested.

'But it's still very Irish,' they told me. 'Why not write something like *Corporal Jack*?' (That book had concerned a German dog attached to an Irish regiment in the British army, fighting Germans in France.)

PART ONE: FICTION

I met Anne Doyle, noted newsreader in RTÉ, and she told me to send the book to their drama department. Presently I got a letter saying that they liked the synopsis and two chapters I'd sent, and decided it would be suitable for a 'made for TV drama'. All the signs seemed favourable, but then they phoned me,

'It's too English. You need to move the middle bit to Ireland.'

As I hadn't preserved the original 'middle bit', I set to work to try to restore it and finally sent it off.

'That's better,' they said, 'but who are your sponsors?'

'My what?'

'Who is financing you?'

'I hoped you were.'

'You must be joking. Contact a few film companies.'

I did, and they said, 'But who's paying?'

It's back in that drawer now.

The commonest grumble about major publishing firms is that they are unapproachable, impersonal, arrogant. This hasn't been my experience. Collins didn't give me a launch, but they did send a nice bunch of flowers and I'm not complaining.

The fact is that big firms pay more and are more likely to get you extra rights. My break came when *Reader's Digest* published *No Harp Like My Own* in one of their condensed books, sharing a volume with Dick Francis and two others.

That contract brought me if not riches, more money than all my other books put together until then. I also got to know commissioning editor Nigel Begbie, editor Sue Poulsen, staff

12. GOING IT ALONE

and editors, and visited them all in London. It got me to the dinner where the book was launched in London. Guest speaker was supposed to be Jeffrey Archer, but he didn't turn up and Danielle Smith spoke at short notice.

Another thing to thank *Reader's Digest* for is a free week in Taormina in Sicily, doing a writing course for a busload of enthusiasts. That was a wonderful week for me. It happened by chance. It was a slow morning in my daughter's antique shop and nothing came in the post except *Reader's Digest*. Thumbing through it I saw an advertisement for a 'Writing holiday in sunny Sicily, plus classes in Italian cooking and photography.' Thinking how much I'd like to go and that I couldn't spare the time or the money for a holiday, I read the small print at the bottom. And snatched up the phone and rang London and said, 'If your writing tutor breaks a leg, I could do that job.'

'Hold on …'

I couldn't believe it when someone picked up and asked me why he thought my name was familiar. I mentioned *No Harp Like My Own*. 'Our tutor hasn't broken his leg,' said the voice, 'but his wife has left him and he wants to get out of the trip.' A few weeks later, I was sitting on a sunny terrace, under a palm tree beside a pool, talking to twenty-six delightful people. I tutored them for an hour a day for a week and seldom enjoyed a holiday more. It certainly didn't seem like work. I'd been told the numbers would fall off – 'they always do', but no, they increased.

When it was time to go home, they gave me presents. I

was astonished. Wine, chocolates, books, make-up and more wine. I had to buy another suitcase.

'This is all very interesting, but how do I approach a publisher?' you might reasonably ask.

Research is the answer (told you it was boring). Given that you don't have published friends to advise you, either get the *Writers' & Artists' Year Book* or consult the Internet where you will find lists of publishers.

Read the particulars of each one with care and make a short list. Nowadays, there is far more information than before. It shouldn't be possible for you to waste time in contacting firms that don't want to know. Also, there are many more allowable ways of presenting your work. Some will consider a preliminary query by e-mail. A great timesaver, this. Make a list and do be certain that the firm you are approaching would at least be interested in a first book.

There's nothing to stop you sending preliminary enquiries to several publishers at a time, in fact you should. E-mails are generally answered quickly. Delete the negative replies and make a shorter list. Be thorough, be prompt, be professional.

Then comes the posting of the manuscript or part of it and the wait and the hopes and fears, until replies arrive. Never post any part of a manuscript uninvited. Chances are you won't get it back. The spectre of rejection may be lurking at your shoulder. Ignore it. Make your covering letter and submission as good as you can.

Sending in a submission, having read everything you can find on the subject, is rather like an interview, when you are sent acres of print on how to dress (modish but restrained), how to speak (briefly and clearly) and how to move (don't unless you have to). This is an exercise in selling yourself, or hiring yourself out, and it sums up your book proposal too. In a word: professionalism. It's a good idea to make sure that the publishers you are sending your manuscript to are likely to be interested: no point sending chick lit to an academic publishers. It's never a bad thing to call up beforehand and find out who to address the cover letter to. 'Dear John Smith' is much better that 'Dear Sir or Madam'. It shows you have done your homework and that you care!

Rejection

This is a negative concept like all those words full of the letter 's'. Depression, recession, pessimism, impossible … that's enough. Don't talk about rejections with anybody but your agent or publisher. Rejection? What's that? Remember you are writing because you want and need to. Persist. Learn.

You must learn to suppress your artistic instincts for a while and become somebody with something to sell. I've often thought that this angle is neglected in writing courses. It's no use sitting at a computer for months, producing something unique, peculiar to you and likely to be valuable, if you aren't going to make a push to sell it. Now you have progressed from the art and craft of writing to the trade and it's every bit as important if your work is to end up in the bookshops.

Many beginners send to one agent and one publisher at a

PART ONE: FICTION

time. This is fine if you have several years free to await results. The process is slow enough without slowing it up further. You wouldn't go about selling a car or some silver like this. You would advertise or put it in an auction. For too many years writers have been schooled to offer their wares cautiously, apologetically, to one august house at a time.

You must remember that most publishers are being swamped with proposals, only a small proportion of which are even going to be read. Again, read the requirements carefully. 'No unsolicited submissions' means what it says. Don't send great bulging parcels of manuscript to anyone unless you have been asked for it. It's slow, expensive and the road to rejection.

You must put aside the feeling that, because your book came from you, again rather like having a baby, it's a personal part of you. It isn't, any more than the cake you baked or the curtains you made. If you are prepared to offer this unique part of yourself to be checked, analysed and possibly rejected by strangers, you are not going to be happy. Not even if you get a yes vote. No, you must grit your teeth and try to look on your precious work as something you want to sell. Something you must sell in order to justify writing more books.

So swallow your pride and consider what you are offering. You have produced something unique, deserving to be read by thousands of people, you say. Well, maybe, but please don't be too intimate with it or you really will suffer when it is turned down. A rejection isn't necessarily a sign of failure. It may be caused by the arrival of a similar book by a better-

12. GOING IT ALONE

known author, a heavy day in the office, a blip in the economy and anything else you can think of beyond your control. So if you get rejections, consider the following names:

>Ernest Hemingway
>Rudyard Kipling
>Leonid Tolstoy
>Stephen King
>Bernard Shaw
>Edgar Allan Poe
>Virginia Woolf
>James Joyce
>Samuel Beckett
>Roddy Doyle

All of these were rejected, some of them many times and overcame it. Some self-published their rejected books, none of them lost heart and gave up. Fortunately. Even that great staple of the self-help books, *Chicken Soup for the Soul*, was turned down a number of times.

Another notable writer, William Golding, was disappointed when his debut novel, *Lord of the Flies*, was rejected. These are just a few and there are dozens of other examples.

Rejection – don't let it get to you. Don't make excuses for not trying again, just get on with your next book. Who said, 'Failure is the opportunity to try again, more intelligently?' I can't remember, but it's true. You can and should try to find out why you were rejected. Often it will have been a mistake to contact this publisher in the first place. This is why I say send your work to several publishers. Don't worry – they are unlikely all to say yes (if they do, you have an auction, but that is outside the scope of this book).

Congratulate yourself for not being tempted to try writing full-time. What is painful for the budding writer with limited time could mean disaster for a full-time pro.

Self-publishing

This isn't often an option in fiction. It has a place in non-fiction, as I will show later. It's madness to employ an agent if you self publish and madness to self-publish if you have an agent.

In Victorian times, gentlemen of leisure wrote – no, penned – long novels. It may have been thought a little bit vulgar to send your work to a publisher; at all events, they avoided the pangs of rejection by giving tremendous dinner parties to celebrate the birth of their books. Full of champagne, the guests lined up with hefty cheques, to sponsor the novel, which would appear in leather binding and marbled endpapers, with their names listed at the beginning.

Acceptance

I've heard people who ought to know better lecturing eager beginners about rejection and acceptance. The general idea is that you get rejections until you could 'paper a room with them' – I don't know why anyone would want to, but this phrase is

12. GOING IT ALONE

popular – and then ... *then*! Your book is accepted and you laugh all the way to the bank and live happily ever after.

Well, no, it's not like that. You get a letter of acceptance, usually hedged about with ifs and buts and terms for a contract are suggested. This is where an agent comes in: you hand over to him or her. I don't want to talk about contracts here, because I'd have so much to repeat in the non-fiction section. You'll find contracts, copyright, libel and so on at the end of the book. But some aspects of book production are different for fiction.

You may be the kind of person who just doesn't want to know about the business aspect of being published. You hate figures and your publisher is in another country. You are miserable because you couldn't find an agent. It isn't too late to look for one (and much easier) once you can say that a certain publisher is interested.

If your book is topical, it may be rushed into print, because books don't stay topical and it might miss the boat. An unknown writer is unlikely to be rushed anywhere. You may sit at home wondering what's happening, perhaps harrying your agent or the publishers who are ignoring you. It's a better idea to ask an established writer what's likely to be happening. Probably not much. Books appear at certain seasons and publishers try to get them out in groups so as to save on publicity and marketing. They market your book and they market you.

It helps the publisher if you are an articulate person and they certainly like authors to be young (so do agents) just as one would prefer to buy a young horse. If the first book is a success, they want to get the maximum number of novels into print while the author is still mobile and more or less sane. It helps if the female author is beautiful, with a mellifluous voice. Look no further than Naomi Campbell and Kate Moss. Failing this, a writer with a good old scandal behind them, or even a prison sentence, gets more attention from the media that a quiet, self-effacing person.

Sad but true. Don't expect that you will automatically get a launch and a book signing at Eason's. These things are designed to make money through publicity, not to make a fuss of the author, or only as an afterthought.

You will have seen the jacket design and the publisher's editor will have done some work on most novels. You will be asked about dedications and acknowledgments. You will have read the proofs and received your free copies. That could be that for a while, except that you should have received an advance. This is normally calculated to cover the royalties on a first printing.

Publication can be anti-climatic. Or it can be wonderful. If the book catches on and the reviews are good, you can have a great time. This could happen with non-fiction too, of course. My own *Breakfast the Night Before,* a memoir, got me three full pages in the London *Times* Saturday Supplement and was briefly a bestseller in England and Ireland.

Don't imagine that once your book is accepted you can leave everything to your publisher, especially if you don't have an agent. The publisher will have asked you for 'biog notes',

12. GOING IT ALONE

as much about your personal life as your writing, may have asked for a photo for the back of the jacket, may have consulted you about a blurb. But you are a new writer; you are unknown. Don't do as I did when *Corporal Jack* was coming out: sit back and wait for nice things to happen. They might. Usually they don't.

If you wait until your book is out to think about publicity, you have waited too long. Your publisher isn't psychic. How is he or she to know that this first-time writer from, say, Leitrim, is a niece or nephew of Patrick Kavanagh, a cousin of Maeve Binchy, a close friend of John Banville? I didn't mention my relationship to Edith Somerville and Anya Seton among others, never thought of it. 'What the hell were you thinking about?' said a young person in publicity.

It's time to stop being a shrinking violet, if that is what you are. You want to go on writing, don't you? Well, then. Make sure that this chance to establish yourself isn't wasted. The shelf-life of the majority of first novels is pitifully short. If yours is remaindered after a couple of months, you will have lost a chance to jump in and get another book accepted on the strength of a synopsis and a couple of chapters.

You don't need to organize publicity yourself, but you do need to tell your publisher anything at all that you think might help sales. In bigger houses, you will have a person assigned to you, whom you can approach with ideas. My problem was that Collins overawed me, culchie that I am. I kept my head down. Anyway, I couldn't go to London when I liked. My husband had died, my daughter was at school, I simply

PART ONE: FICTION

couldn't get away. I never did meet my agent in Edinburgh.

Something you might do is to make a list of people in the media who are known to you, if any. They will print a press release and occasionally a review. Anyone in the national newspapers will be sent a review copy and some publicity material. This kind of advertisement is cheap. Your publishers will send out review copies as routine, but it's good to have a name to send them to. Get your friends to help. With enough pushing and shoving at the beginning, your book should do as well as it's capable of doing.

A final few words. If anyone asks you if you are writing another book, say 'Yes,' even if you have only made some sketchy notes. Keep writing, because if your first book is a success, you won't get much warning. After the normal slow start for a first novel, it just might suddenly take off. You should be halfway through the next one. Don't be caught without an idea in your head when your publisher asks for a follow-up.

PART TWO

Non-Fiction

13. The Same but Different

Much of the first part of this book applies to non-fiction as well. The most closely related category to fiction is memoir, including biography and autobiography. At the other extreme are all the how-to books, self-help, mind body and spirit, health, history, war, religion, education, local interest, travel, sport, pets, cookery, gardening, arts and crafts, and a great many subdivisions of these.

It is easier to get a toe in the door with non-fiction because the fiction market is so limited. Fact is always with us. Think of the millions of newspapers and magazines that crowd the newsagents' shelves; the radio programmes that go on all day and all night; the thirst so many of us have to gather information on a chosen subject. Non-fiction is life itself. The opportunities are endless.

In my own case, fact and fiction intertwined, as I milked various ideas for different markets with some success.

PART TWO: NON-FICTION

Looking along the bookshop shelves, I wonder how long this book would be if it had to embrace all these categories. *Looking After Your Pet Snake*, *Surfing in a Simulator* (a what?), *Success at Scrabble*, *Beautiful Toenails*, *Showing Guinea Pigs for Pleasure* (yes I promise you). I noted these titles down a few years back for an article; you might be too late, but perhaps if you really need them, there might be some still in print.

When you get the urge to write a novel, look forward to a longish wait before it appears in the shops, even if your debut book is written, edited and published at the first submission without a major hitch. Not likely, but I suppose it happens sometimes. Non-fiction, though, can be a vague idea on Monday and in the shops on Friday. Because writing for your local paper is the surest way to start.

We're back with 'How I did it,' now, as I have had a lot of material published over the years and have made some money, enjoyed myself and learned a great deal. As I have written two memoirs about my own life, I may have to repeat myself, but you'll just have to put up with that.

An accidental writer

When I was writing small unpaid pieces for *Working Sheepdog News*, which later bore fruit with my first book of fiction, *One Dog and His Man*, the editor asked me for a piece about sheepdog trials in Ireland. I sent in some trial results and a short piece about Martin O'Neill, a leading sheepdog handler at the time and for many years afterwards.

13. THE SAME BUT DIFFERENT

They asked for more results, which was easy as I was at a trial most Sundays all summer long. I was 'writing what I knew' and although I don't always agree with that saying, so boring and flat-footed, in novel writing, I can't emphasize it too much if you write for the press on a specialized subject.

Horses had been my life for decades, and I'd been breeding and training Border Collies for several years before I began writing about them. It did cross my mind that I should be writing about horses, perhaps even getting paid for it, but thousands of other people were already doing that. Sheepdogs, their care and training, were little written about. The people in those days, who trained and handled dogs on the land and at trials, were mostly of the strong, silent type.

Did I say silent? I've heard some of them admonishing or encouraging their dogs from a distance of half a mile or so ... I'll withdraw 'silent'. In the late Seventies, we had about twenty dogs on the farm, four completely trained, plus young dogs, pups and four breeding bitches. The dogs with the Crannagh prefix were well known; their bloodlines are carried today by a host of winners as well as honest-to-goodness farm dogs. Proof of this was our ready market for pups, many being ordered before they had been conceived, never mind born. I had a complete set of studbooks and a number of extremely knowledgeable and successful friends. I knew my subject pretty well.

I thought I'd save time and trouble by writing a little handout for customers called *Looking After Your Sheepdog Pup*, so that I could give a copy to everyone that bought one and they would get useful information on rearing and training. I showed it to my husband to make sure I hadn't made any silly mistakes and he said, 'It's good. Send it to *Farmers Journal*.'

Today, I know one is supposed to send a preliminary letter. Mind you, I don't. You will be lucky to get an answer and will have wasted two stamps. E-mail is safer. Then you should have studied the paper and know exactly who to ask for. You ring reception and ask for this person by name, giving your own as if you expected the secretary to have heard of you. In 1982, I didn't know anything. I went straight to the phone and rang the paper, asking the lady who replied how I could get an article published in the home pages. 'You want Quentin Doran O'Reilly,' she said, 'he's a dote.'

She put me through, I told Quentin what I'd written and read a paragraph to him.

He said, 'We need something like that' – I nearly fainted – 'could you stretch it to a series of six articles, about 600 words, called "The Farm Dog"? Would £25 suit you? Right. Send the first article along as soon as you like.' They don't come any dotier than that.

These words had as much effect on me as the acceptance of any of my books. Easy! Of course I could. I sent off the (handwritten) articles and after the third he raised my fee to £30. When I'd finished the series, I got a good deal of mail, mostly flattering, which told me I was onto something profitable. I put the articles together, added a few photos and asked Gleesons' Printers in Nenagh to print me a little book, *The Farm Dog: a Beginner's Guide*. I sold 500 copies in very

13. THE SAME BUT DIFFERENT

little time, another 500 over a year or two and 200 more over a longer interval. They were doubling their money, an unusual thing for a booklet to do.

This may seem a lot of angst about nothing much. If you think that writing unpaid for a specialist magazine is starting at the bottom of the ladder, you are wrong. It's straining to reach the bottom rung. But I was learning that whatever happened, I could earn extra income enjoyably with very little trouble. I wrote a series for young people on the same subject for *Irish Farmers Monthly* and went back to the *Journal* with a fortnightly column on problems with farm dogs. I got ambitious and sent something to the British *Farmer & Stockbreeder*. They took it and asked for more.

I looked forward to the fan mail that the paper sent to me every week. It included flattery, yes, orders for my booklet, even an offer of marriage. Then there were the usual cranks and one man who said I should be at home minding my children. 'I know your sort,' he said, and I wondered if he did. Startled at first by some of the content, I got used to my unlikely pen friends and made a couple of good friends who were sheepdog enthusiasts too.

The reason for this easy path to a handy second income was that I had no competition in Ireland and very little in the UK. When I began to get short of material, I turned to subsistence sheep farming. People who were in sheep in a big way were never my target, but I had run miles after my few ewes, then acquired a good dog and left the running to him. I knew his value. I sold articles in sets of six to various sources:

PART TWO: NON-FICTION

'Sheep on the Cheap', 'Lambs without Tears', 'Farming with Dog and Stick'. I'd added the *Sheep Farmer*, a Welsh magazine, to my list of publications, as well as *Sheepdogs*, an American production whose editor, Carole Presberg, co-wrote a book with me in 1998.

Soon I was writing occasional features for *Farming Independent* and travelling to trials, sheep-shearing contests and the Ploughing Championship to interview winners. At that time I was working on *Corporal Jack*, with two more books lined up. I could have taken up authorship combined with freelance journalism full-time. The truth is I got bored with writing for newspapers and magazines, although one way and another, they paid better than books over my first few years. I wanted to give more time to writing novels.

I learned some valuable lessons when writing for the press. I had always been active and inclined to be restless when obliged to keep still. I found the enforced solitude and stillness more difficult than the writing and would use any excuse to roam about restlessly. I never had a great deal of time to waste roaming about, so had to teach myself to sit still and write. When I got used to it, I found that I wrote more fluently if I set a time for myself, not more than an hour, but I stuck to it. If I'd sat down to write my first novel in my restless days and thought about the sheer bulk of 100,000 words, I'd have been tempted to give up.

My agent, David Fletcher, asked if I'd anything else to offer and I sent him *The Farm Dog*. Within a week or two, I had a commission to write *All About the Working Border*

13. THE SAME BUT DIFFERENT

Collie, a handsome illustrated hardback, for Pelham Books, a subsidiary of Penguin. That was an easy book to write and quickly finished.

The downside was that most writers are mentally labelled by their readers and I was clearly labelled *dog*. Marginally better than *sheep*, I thought, but it was hard to escape from the rut I'd so painstakingly dug for myself. I've told how I introduced a guide dog into a novel to please my publishers and they informed me that I could be another Joyce Stranger, when I was desperate to shake off my dog label.

The Pelham book was reprinted every year until the series was discontinued, about ten years, then TFH in the States bought it updated and without the 'All About' tag, with a section about Collies in the USA by Carole Presberg. By that time I could claim to be an established writer in my field (literally) but I was getting bored with that particular field. I turned to my horse-dealing experiences and had a winter column in *The Irish Field* for many years. These articles formed the base for my memoirs, *Breakfast the Night Before*, and *Saturday's Child*.

My boss in the *Field* was Grania Willis, who encouraged me enormously, and later Marie Claire Digby. It was good working for them. It also got me an annual invitation to a splendid boozy lunch at Castletown House. Years later, it led to being asked to write a 25,000-word section in the *History of the Irish Draught*, edited by Mary McGrath and published by Collins of Cork, which was fun to write and popular with readers.

So you see, one thing leads to another and there has to be something that you are knowledgeable about and could write about entertainingly. This is the niche market, where an ordinary person with an informed interest in something unusual can blossom as a writer. I'll get back to the horsy bit later. Horses aren't a niche, but a vast subject, sprouting in every direction. My angle was not that I rode them, but that I bought and sold them and by so doing was able to keep the farm I would otherwise have had to sell. And that was the selling point.

The problem with a tiny niche is that when it gets over-filled, as it will, you need an alternative, so think ahead and have something ready. Editors, like publishers, are reluctant to let writers escape from their comfortable niches.

Training

I don't intend to start examining different college opportunities, because my part-time writer couldn't spare the time and might not have the inclination to work for specialized qualifications. A young person leaving school would probably aim for a degree from a College of Journalism or Technical College. Learning journalism by this method has practical aspects. The student can practise news reporting, interviews and feature writing while studying. This will teach them a lot about editors and work procedures before they start. But the beauty of journalism as a part-time occupation is that you can start without any qualifications whatsoever, provided you have

13. THE SAME BUT DIFFERENT

something interesting to say and can get it down on paper.

You need a particular make up to be a successful news reporter, as well as professional training, but you might discover an aptitude for feature writing or radio work.

If you are shy, squeamish, thin-skinned or an introvert, forget investigative journalism. It doesn't mean that you have nothing to say. Perhaps you express yourself beautifully: there is a place for most people who can write well. But it would be silly to expose yourself to the near libellous criticism that follows almost any report on a disaster or crime.

There are far more opportunities than ever before. New radio stations appear, new cable television programmes come and go, the choice widens all the time. The internet, especially, provides a whole new medium for poeple who want to get their stories read. You could also work as a columnist for a local newspaper on an occasional basis. It wouldn't make you rich, but it would provide valuable experience, a small wage and perhaps a stepping stone to a national daily or a popular tabloid.

The bottom rung and climbing

There's no reason why anyone with a day job shouldn't ease into a few articles on the side, thence to a column and then to a memoir, as I did. All you need is the subject and a strong desire to write about it.

I was a speaker at the opening of a writers' group, about ten years ago and a woman asked me how she could make a few pounds out of writing. She wanted to write, but couldn't afford the risks and the waiting associated with the publication of books.

I asked her if she had a special interest and she said she hadn't, but someone else said, 'What about your baking?'

'Yes, well, anyone can bake.' I followed it up and discovered that she baked cakes and scones, fast, professionally and well, making a small extra income. I suggested that she try sharing her expertise by writing a cookery column with the emphasis on an extra money-earner with a low outlay. In no time at all, she landed a cookery column with a newspaper and kept it for years. Then she got such a demand for her cakes and buns that she gave up writing about them.

On another occasion, I had been giving a talk about turning a specialized subject to good account and a woman said, 'Well, all I really know about is weeds. I can't write about weeds.' I don't know if she did, but I remarked that weeds are plants, just the ones you don't want, and gardening is one of the most popular subjects in non-fiction. Weed control, eco-friendly or otherwise is a fashionable concern and there are loads of gardening magazines as well as gardening sections in magazines. And she could branch out and write a whodunit featuring weed-killer.

'How?' somebody wanted to know.

'She could have a clean green heroine who confiscates weedkiller from a vengeful gardener. Somebody dies. Traces of Roundup found at post-mortem, lean, clean-limbed hero suspected ... betrayal ... heroine's exhaustive knowledge of

13. THE SAME BUT DIFFERENT

vegetable poisoning saves the day.' Over the top, I thought. But no, after the session, someone asked if he could use the plot.

This was an example of specialist writing for the media expanding into a main character and theme for a novel, just as my dog-related writing overflowed and was the basis, not merely of three 'how-to' books, but of two successful novels.

Remember, knowledge is fine, but of no interest unless you are interested yourself. If your special knowledge was acquired painfully and slowly, the chances are that your writing on the subject will be painful and slow. You need enthusiasm for your subject if you are going to share it with others and you must convey your enthusiasm to the printed page. It can be done. Without it you have a manual, not a book.

Assuming that you have a small niche subject you feel you could write about, how do you begin? Don't say, 'By taking a diploma course in journalism as a mature student,' because that brings you back to seeking a fresh career. You already have a career, or a way of life. You don't need a profession, although in the years ahead, who knows?

Let's say you are a whiz at tracing peoples' roots. This is one of those pursuits that require a good knowledge of using the Internet, and a large proportion of people, anxious to discover their roots but not computer-minded, have to put letters in the papers, advertise or pay for research. I've chosen this subject because I searched for lots of roots for American and Australian people and it is a popular theme.

First, you should check any specialist magazines concerned with emigrants and see what sort of thing they print.

Then contact the most hopeful and offer a few short articles about different families, originally from your part of the world, now flourishing in distant parts of the globe.

The reason for jumping straight in with a sales pitch for several articles is that a series suits the small-press editor, who will keep a space for it, probably no more than once a month. You might be offered a tiny amount of money, but like the short stories you use as practice for writing novels, you are going to be writing something and clearing your costs at least. If it leads nowhere, think of something else.

When you write for the media, whether it's a knitting magazine or the *Financial Times*, you have to remember a few rules:

Be methodical.
Be punctual.
Be reliable.
Don't argue unless you must.

Present your work tidily, using good quality paper, clean folders and white envelopes if you post your work in, although these days most places will only accept submissions by e-mail. Dont' forget to include your details, e-mail address or return address, with your material. And make it look tidy. I haven't forgotten being in an editor's office where he showed me an article typed on lined paper in a brown envelope with an assortment of postmarks and labels.

'If you treat your copy like shit,' he said, 'why should anyone else value it?'

13. THE SAME BUT DIFFERENT

Give it your best shot always and try not to mind the editorial interference you are likely to get; not to mention the letters from people complaining because you have found a sheep-stealer or worse in their ancestry.

I got on well with the staff in the *Farmer's Journal* and *The Irish Field* because they knew I would deliver copy on time. Later, I had a good relationship with publishers for a similar reason; I could be relied on to respect deadlines.

Let's say that you are doing nicely with your 'roots' articles. Look around for a more upmarket publication that might like a one-off article, leading to questions from readers. Progressing cautiously, you may find yourself a couple of rungs higher. And everything you write is going into your CV or biog notes. 'Writes regularly for specialist journals,' sounds better than 'Occasional contributor to *Your Irish Roots*.'

It's no use being thin-skinned if you plan to write for the press. You must thicken it somehow or suffer. Editors have no time for sensitive souls and sub-editors even less. It's the best training you could possibly get, once you've got used to having your precious work cut and slashed, given a new title, put back three weeks or simply not printed at all.

You learn to write short sentences with crystal-clear meanings. You learn to write the exact number of words you were asked for. Three hundred words doesn't mean 320. Send 320 and expect to see a whole paragraph lopped off.

I was lucky because my local papers were and are the *Nenagh Guardian* and *Tipperary Star*. Both treated me with friendly consideration.

PART TWO: NON-FICTION

There's a tendency in city dwellers to think you need to live in a city to work for a newspaper. Again, the career reporter does best where there are plenty of people doing interesting or illegal things. A freelance in a small town can do nicely. If you keep your eyes and ears open, you can find copy in places where the nationals don't go. A little-known area could launch a successful career.

Working for and with the local press should give you experience, confidence and a new sense of proportion. And the odd laugh. In one local paper I saw the following under 'items for sale': 'For bed sitter read red setter.'

Earlier, writing about fiction, I urged you to find comfortable times for writing, in line with your own normal schedule. I warned that you could spend half of your fixed time staring dismally at the screen without a coherent thought in your head. Write when you want and need to write. Do your thinking beforehand. Let your unconscious mind process your ideas and deliver them when you need them. Remember how you daydreamed as a child. Almost every writer has been a daydreamer. How you abandoned the dream only in order to eat or sleep and how you picked up the threads at the next opportunity with a clutch of fresh ideas thrown in.

Writing articles is different. Easier in most ways, because they are brief and you always have guidelines as to length and slant on the subject. But your deadline may not be generous. There are throngs of eager, literate people out there, with time on their hands who would love to write articles. Don't let them. As soon as you know the required length and

13. THE SAME BUT DIFFERENT

subject of the material, sit down and write a short outline. Then finish it as soon as you can. The main reason is that the subject although familiar, may bore you through its very familiarity. Sit down. Write it. It shouldn't take long. You can leave that particular brand of journalism when you have something more interesting going. With your competence you earn the editor's respect, so you can progress to choosing your own subject, or new angle on an old subject. Then you are in charge again and the writing will flow.

Even then, don't be tempted to send in an extra fifty words. Edit your article with a hard head and heavy hand: you won't regret it. Journalists can't spread themselves, any more than novelists can compress their nicely timed and spaced writing.

When I was writing for *The Irish Field*, it was for the 'half-bred' section, rather than the racing and breeding that comprised most of the paper. This was edited by Valentine Lamb and was no concern of mine. Then one day, he phoned and said that (I think) Leopardstown had been rained or frozen off and he needed a minimum of 1000 words at short notice.

'What about?'

'Horses. Racing – what do you think?'

'Yes, but …'

'A story, something about the National; that's next week, I want it tonight.' He hung up. I had no e-mail in those days, no fax. I lived five miles from town. I phoned the office and got a helpful girl. 'You'll have to put it on the train,' she said, 'send it to Heuston Station and we'll get it picked up.' It was lucky I was familiar with my subject. It was then about three o'clock. I believe Kevin Myers went to fetch it and it duly appeared the next day. This happened on a couple of other occasions, so I had a few outlines by me to write up if needed. That first deadline was a nightmare I won't forget. Later on, this kind of challenge was exciting. I knew I could do it and there was no panic.

I should mention here that editors have their own ideas about titles for articles and about illustrations. Don't protest, as you won't be heeded and you must avoid being known as a moaner.

Your local paper might accept an interview from you. Interviews are good, provided the persons interviewed are amenable and likeable, the very devil if they aren't. They can also give you a useful boost.

If you hear that a native of your town has done something remarkable and you hear it in good time, suggest that you might do an interview. Of course, the person in question has to be asked too. An interview generally requires a photograph. Sometimes the person interviewed supplies one, sometimes the newspaper sends a photographer.

When you write articles that concern people rather than things, get somebody to give an opinion on the subject. Somebody, that is, with knowledge of the person. Then ask if you can quote them in an article. If the response is negative, don't persist, find somebody else. This isn't interview writing exactly, but it's good practice in getting somebody to give an opinion other than your own, with reasons.

13. THE SAME BUT DIFFERENT

A 'proper' interview would be done at the person's house or in a public place. Hotel lounges aren't ideal, but are often the easiest places to organize. Use a recorder, I beg. When I was interviewing sheep-shearers and the like in the 1980s, there was nothing between a mini-recorder and a solid arrangement of tapes and leads, which sat on the table whirring, putting me off as well as the other person and of course, no use out of doors.

The biggest reason for recording instead of taking notes is that although many journalists do take notes, you need to quote and you must do it accurately or not at all.

'Mary Smith is delighted with her success. "I didn't expect anything like this," she says …' This popular format brings an interview alive, but if you are relying on notes, you should read the quote back to the person. Established journalists are less fussy.

' "I'm over the moon about my new book", says Marjorie, as she sips her favourite tipple by the turf fire.' That's what the newspaper printed, but those aren't my words and the 'tipple' was a cup of tea.

If your interviews are popular and the feedback is good, you might be asked to interview a celebrity, but please think twice if they are known for being late, rude or hypersensitive. Ask yourself if you, a harmless part-time writer, got the job because nobody on the staff of the paper would touch it.

14. Memoir and Biography

The genre of non-fiction nearest to the novel is memoir or biography. You don't write a biography of *anyone* without exhaustive knowledge, written permission, access to further information and a worthy subject. You have to be a good writer indeed to transcend your subject if he or she is a charismatic public figure. Such books are generally commissioned – the authorized biography of some politician or other … you've seen them in the libraries and they are heavy-going as a rule, the commissioned author being closely watched by family and friends for even a hint that the subject might have been less than perfect.

Snapping at the heels of authorized biographers are the Kitty Kelleys and the like, all lined up for a share of the carcass. This group includes some wildly successful but not admirable people, most of them newspaper reporters or journalists with

14. MEMOIR AND BIOGRAPHY

access to anything defamatory they can get away with. This is not an option for the part-timer, even if you knew the departed luminary intimately, had enjoyed a passionate affair with them, lent them money, saved them from drink and drugs or drowning ... it won't do. First, you would let a crowd of dubious characters into your life. You might be asked, then pestered to sell information, you might be threatened. Whatever happened, you would never get that book into print without the expensive help of lawyers. Not a suitable genre for most of us.

Of course if you had been married to the person, if you'd had a child together, lived together for years, you just might have a big seller on your hands, but be prepared to lose most of your friends and to acquire heavyweight enemies. Don't go there.

Memoir has just about taken over from autobiography, which is mainly confined to elderly politicians and retired generals. I take it you are neither, so forget autobiography until you have large quantities of suitable material and a couple of secretaries. Your memoir could be a viable option, so I'll concentrate on that.

It's important to ask yourself a few questions before you start. The biggest and least pleasant is, 'Are people going to want to read about me?' Be honest. Are they? There are choices here. If your own doings are interesting in themselves, that's a start. Or did you take part in some famous movement, witness a frightful disaster? Are you or were you intimate with somebody who did? Another person's life can be the most important thing in your memoir.

PART TWO: NON-FICTION

This is a type of authorship that depends less on publication than fiction does. I have edited at least a dozen books of memoirs and just a few of the authors were hell-bent on big money and publicity. Some didn't even want to publish, but did want a tidy job, well presented, giving all the facts, as a memento for their families. Memoir is easier to place than a novel but, like any other writing, it needs a purpose. When its purpose is to save people and events from oblivion, entirely for the sake of the author's family, self-publishing is a sensible option. You can get as many books printed as you think you can sell, throw a big party and feel you have done something worthwhile. There is always the lurking feeling too, that you might be forgotten when you die. It is natural to prefer to be remembered.

When I started to write a memoir myself, I used the articles about horse-fairs I'd printed in *The Irish Field* as a backbone. Milking an idea again most successfully. I had no claims to fame, but had made my living out of buying and selling horses, which is usually thought to be a good way of going broke. I'd started with £50 and had hundreds of horses through my hands, some of them well known, over about thirty-five years.

My beginnings hadn't suggested anything of the kind as I was a pampered child with a nanny, while later I was a tomboy running wild. The book succeeded because it was light-hearted and people could empathize with me. The first-person singular makes for easy reading and it is a real memoir, written as I remembered things that happened a long time

14. MEMOIR AND BIOGRAPHY

ago. Again the memoir writer is a storyteller, a *Seanachaí* offering entertainment, so if you talk well and can keep a number of people interested, you'll manage.

You 'tell' from a character's viewpoint in a novel, from your own in a memoir. Here, you can use your own voice, which is out of place in fiction, except perhaps in children's stories. In a novel, your voice, mannerisms and tricks of speech might be given to one character, but not to everyone. Memoir has only one voice except in dialogue.

The dreaded writer's block is less likely to occur when you write about yourself, you are inwardly telling your own story to a few friends as you write, so you won't dry up, any more than you would suddenly become tongue-tied in the middle of a conversation. You may be at a loss for a suitable word and here writing is easier than talking. I leave a blank or a query and go back and do a bit of tweaking if I'm not happy with a word or phrase.

André Deutsch brought my memoir out in hardback and Diana Athill was unimpressed by my fear and dislike of being on TV. 'Don't be silly,' she said. So it happened that I sat shivering with nerves, in a dark passage, watching Pat Kenny interviewing Milo O'Shea. I'd like to be able to say that, once on stage the nerves left me. They didn't. I was cold with fright. But I haven't had a problem with public appearances since.

Avoid writing the type of book that is a straight run through of your life to the present day. Such a work might be a valuable record for your family, but unless you are quite

PART TWO: NON-FICTION

extraordinary, a publisher isn't likely to get over-excited about it.

You need to highlight certain aspects of your life. Maybe it is your unusual work, your strange experiences in some remote country, your unique experiences during some horrifying set of circumstances or how you came to terms with illness or a disability. Any kind of experience has possibilities as long as it's fairly unusual and will keep the reader interested.

From the start, decide what emotions you want to provoke in your readers. Do you want them to be fascinated, frightened, totally gutted, amusingly entertained, puzzled, angered, envious or even repelled? Have you got a book in you strong enough to carry a reader through to the end? Amusing enough to make them smile as they read? Horrifying enough to make them warn their friends?

A memoir that deals solely with your career isn't likely to interest many outside your own circle of friends; publishers are unlikely to be impressed unless your occupation is in a popular field like sport or drama. Be careful if the subject was topical when you first thought about it. Nothing is more tedious than an account of a craze that didn't last.

You can be miserable if you like. There's always been a market for miserable rural childhoods; Frank McCourt popularized miserable urban childhoods and a number of people have written about miserable boyhoods and girlhoods at the mercy of Christian Brothers or sadistic nuns. You can write about your work for charity or among destitute people and as long as you are genuine your book will be read. Only write

14. MEMOIR AND BIOGRAPHY

what you feel strongly about. Attempts to beef up your own emotions are likely to fail.

Much depends, of course, on the quality of your writing. If it is exceptional, that quality may be enough to carry a slender thread of events through to the end and still be gripping. Average writing needs above average material and vice versa.

There are hundreds of memoirs written by elderly people, telling of how it was in the old days. We are getting back to the comely maidens and dancing at the crossroads here, for the eye of love as we know is blind, or at least selective. It's a personal dislike of mine, reading about all those contented people living in their thatched cottages without a care in the world. I remember those times too well – the sicknesses and deaths from TB of children and young people, the overcrowded rooms, the overflowing families. Yes, people were happy, but in spite of the lives they led rather than because of them. Without emigration their lot would have been even worse.

Write about what you remember, but do check with someone who has experienced those same halcyon cloudless days.

On the whole, I think Irish people are good at writing their memoirs and I have edited work for some real naturals. I hope you are one of them.

The biggest mistake of most beginners is to start as far back as they can remember (or think they remember), and plod steadily through their lives. I've seen so many starting, 'I was born …' Unless you were born in very strange circumstances, this opening is a turn-off. Look for an incident in your life, one that you really remember and start with that. I can remember back to being three years old, but only because a couple of events have stuck in my mind. Others I have spoken to remember little before the age of eight or nine. Don't resort to guesswork or things you have been told by your parents.

Writing a memoir in which you are not the protagonist is different in all sorts of ways. It is nothing like biography, which follows a person's life from the cradle to the grave. It picks out things in the other person's life that you had access to and shared, things that you have remembered with delight – or horror – ever since. In some ways this is easier; you avoid the I, I, I, syndrome and seeming to be self-serving, but inevitably there are snags. Most of these are provided by other people whom you need to consult about your subject.

The actual composition of memoirs is closely related to that of a novel. The points I made in the chapters on fiction also apply. Look back to the section on 'Usage and Abusage' and 'Dialogue'; bear in mind the use of original words and phrases, how to introduce descriptive passages without holding the story up and the use of dialogue. For yes, there is a place for dialogue in your life story. As in the novel, dialogue helps to flesh out a character and moves the plot along. In a three-or four-page account of an event, you really need to break it up from time to time and the spoken word is ideal for this.

14. MEMOIR AND BIOGRAPHY

Here are some good and bad reasons for writing your memoirs:

Good Something extraordinary, but personal to you occurred during your childhood or adolescence and you have genuine information to back up your story in the shape of personal letters and newspaper articles.

Bad Something extraordinary but personal to you happened to you, or a deceased friend of yours during your childhood. Your daddy was always talking about it.

Good Your first novel has been accepted. Your publishers would like another. You can't think of a worthy follow-up, but writing it has reminded you of your childhood and your discovery of all those letters marked 'top secret'.

Bad Your publishers want another novel but you haven't an idea in your head. However, you send off some fascinating memories of childhood holidays at Ballybunion, Tramore and Salthill, complete with funny incidents. People really do write about this kind of thing, pay to get it published and call themselves authors.

Good You have clear memories of your youth and, although the nuns were lovely, the Brothers pleasant and your parents delightful, you have a real gift for making people live, for sparkling dialogue and convincing description.

PART TWO: NON-FICTION

Bad You have clear memories of your idle, boring youth and feel that as many people as possible should share them.

Memoir is not a poor relation of fiction. Boswell's *Life of Johnson* and *Pepys' Diary* have survived for centuries.

In our own time, Brian Keenan's *An Evil Cradling* is a classic in its genre. *Cider with Rosie* is a lovely book; there are hundreds I'd like to name. *The Kon-Tiki Expedition* stood out as an example of its kind back in the Fifties; it's more a travel book than a memoir and travel books are a sort of subdivision of memoir. *A Year in Provence* by Peter Mayle is a more recent instance and Dervla Murphy, while writing a spell-binding memoir, *Wheels Within Wheels*, has excelled in the same field.

The personal memories of the rich and famous are ghosted as often as not and there is room out there for a willing, self-effacing ghost. Look in the advertisements in writing magazines if you are interested, but remember that you get a down payment and that's that. You keep quiet and seek someone else to haunt. I have been asked to ghost a book a couple of times and refused, so I can't provide personal gory details, but I'd met an embittered ghost and didn't want to try it.

A collaboration is fairly common, usually with a family member or a colleague at work. Don't be in a hurry to agree. The family rows caused by shared memories of the same person have caused rifts between friends and relations, while there is often an unseemly squabble about whose name comes first on the title-page and who signs copies.

If you need a collaborator, remember that it's more important for them to be on the same wavelength than to be an authority on the subject. A writing partner who is always a step behind and who couldn't, for example, contribute a few sentences in a style similar to your own, is best forgotten. Get a researcher if you need one instead and do the writing yourself.

Illustrators

Non-fiction is often illustrated. Publishers have their own ideas about illustrations and they may not coincide with yours. When editing memoirs for others, I have often been shown a number of faded photographs of the author's relatives, spouse and children. Should your family be famous and your photographs never seen before, there is a case for including them. Unless this is so, only use photos that are crisp and clear. Old, faded pictures can be restored, but it's expensive if the end product still isn't very good.

As for drawings or paintings, I hardly know how to advise. I illustrated one of my own books with pen and ink drawings and the Farming Press was happy with them, but the earlier editions were illustrated by someone else, as was the edition still in print. There are photographs in another book, but I was asked to supply 'plenty' and wasn't consulted about which were to be used.

Don't forget that photographs and drawings are copyright. You aren't likely to run into trouble, but you should ask permission and acknowledge all photos and drawings.

I used pictures I'd taken myself in the *Working Border Collie* books, also some taken by a leading photographer. I wasn't pleased when I found several of them in another 'doggy' book, neither captioned nor acknowledged.

Writers who have their life stories self-published often illustrate them with grainy snaps that no conventional publisher would consider for a minute. In many cases, I've advised them to get them scanned, cropped and restored, as being more palatable than simply saying, 'They aren't good enough.'

I hate having to say, 'It's not good enough' about anybody's writing. I have seen a shy, sensitive woman cry in public because of harsh criticism of her work. I would always pick on the most positive aspect of the manuscript and discuss that for long enough to relax the writer, then approach the less good areas, combining fair criticism with ideas for bettering it. I can't remember who said, 'Be your own best friend and severest critic,' but it's excellent advice for a writer of memoirs. You need to be kind to yourself, to encourage yourself, for writing is indeed a lonely occupation. But when you reach the end of a chapter and turn to check it for typos, check it severely for quality. This is more pleasant than waiting for a publisher's editor to do it, as you are the person to improve it. For it's your job to make it as perfect as possible.

Finally, do please keep reading whenever you get the chance. I have found that some books feed my urge to write, although I don't know how or why.

14. MEMOIR AND BIOGRAPHY

I have dealt with memoirs at some length, because they are easier to write than novels and, if successful, will outlive most middle-of-the-road novels.

15. How-to and How-not-to

The how-to book is unlikely to make you rich and famous, but it can make you happier and more popular.

In a memoir, you are writing about the person you know best and probably the people you love most as well. In a how-to book, you are writing about the occupation you know best. I've spoken of niche writing and mentioned writing for the press on your best subject. Mine was breeding, training and caring for working Border Collies.

Pelham Books commissioned a book about them and although much of it was history and anecdote, it was packed with information on every aspect of Border Collie management. The book was reprinted again and again and is quoted as a source in a number of similar works. There's no mystique in a book of this kind. It's straightforward information and instruction.

15. HOW-TO AND HOW-NOT-TO

You may not have a favourite subject suitable for explaining in a full-length book. If you have, go for it. It's comparatively easy to find a home for such a book, even if it's a short work about a limited subject. If the publishers of your chosen subject turn you down, go back to the specialist magazines while you consider the next move.

Coffee tables are burdened with enormous volumes entitled grandly, *Painting*, or *Cats*, or *Cars*, which are profusely illustrated and heavy enough to break your toe if you drop one. Those who want to find out more about painting, cats or cars, are likely to turn to smaller, fatter books, which pack a much greater amount of information.

So see if your subject will run to a smaller, fatter book. Do some research to back up what you know or to challenge what you thought you knew. Write a synopsis and sample chapters and try to place it before you write it. You might decide to self-publish and this is one of the areas where it could be a good idea. Say you want to write about canaries. I don't think you would unless you knew a great deal about them, so that's okay for a start. You would go to places where canary fanciers go and meet many like-minded people. Your little book, *All You Need to Know About Canaries*, would be circulated among them and people would buy it. Not thousands, maybe, but possibly hundreds. Then you would be in a better position to offer a big, heavy, profusely illustrated book called *Canaries*, to a specialized publisher, with a good chance of having it accepted.

This is what I did myself: the booklet *The Farm Dog* was

PART TWO: NON-FICTION

enough for Pelham Books to commission *The Working Border Collie*.

It's a good idea to make your how-to book enjoyable to read, but you must order it from the start. Divide it into sections, then into subsections. Use clear photographs and/or diagrams and make all captions crystal clear. The person reading your instructions may be actually performing the activity described. If it's active or risky in any way, they won't have time to winkle the facts out of the fine writing.

I suggest you consult a book about a similar subject, not to copy but to check the format. Some specialist publishers supply a list of requirements.

If your hobby is also part of your livelihood, the book will benefit you by spreading the word. Try to find an ideal picture for the dust jacket and try to get a person well known in the same field to write a foreword. Your book isn't concerned with the art of writing, only the craft. Dedicate it to somebody you admire in the same area and hope your subject doesn't go out of fashion.

I've now dealt with all the kinds of book I've personally written and had published. They account for a fair share of subjects but there are many more. These books are informative without being instructive. You'd love to know everything about some sport or occupation, but not so much that you want to learn how to do it. However, you might well want to teach about it or even write about it yourself, using a different approach. There are endless headings for books like these and all require specialized knowledge.

15. HOW-TO AND HOW-NOT-TO

A great deal of what I've written already applies to specialist books and the first thing you need is exhaustive knowledge of your subject. It would be almost impossible (and very boring) to list the headings. You will find them in the shelves of any bookshop.

Again, you need to be familiar enough with your subject to go on live radio and be questioned about it without the deepest misgivings. Then learn some more. Research, read it up and be very sure there's a market for it and that you really want to write it. It's most important to consider your readership, whether you decide to write about stately homes or scuba diving.

Informative books cover the whole range of readers from the experts, anxious to perfect their knowledge, through students, middlebrows with a mild interest, down to the casual browser. It would be impossible for me to advise on all these, even if I could. The best you can hope for is to appeal to as wide a range of readers as possible.

I'd hesitate to write such a book without positive encouragment from a publisher or agent. Some articles in specialist magazines would help. But what helps most in almost every kind of non-fiction book is the personality and involvement of the writer. Without that, you have a textbook.

Local history

I've left this category until last but, in Ireland anyway, it is a favourite theme and I needed to check out a few details. I'm not going to talk about the kind of work that is written by a historian, because that doesn't come within the compass of this book.

This form of niche writing depends largely on where you live and how much you know and care about your locality. It is mainly of interest to country and village dwellers, but a successful book about your village might lead to something similar about another town or area not far away. I was invited by a British publisher to put a picture book together about my home town, but others had already had the same idea. You should make sure before you start that nobody else is writing about your area.

Like reporting, this is not for the thin-skinned; no matter what you do, you are certain to annoy somebody. If you have lived there for less time than that person, you may be called a blow-in, even if you've lived there thirty years to his forty. I think it would be wise to join the local Historical Society or Heritage Society. Both are likely to be helpful with research. Another big advantage is that some groups may subsidize your book, or guide you to a concern that will. Another thing you can do is to write letters to the editors of local papers, asking for information. Sift it well and use only what can be verified.

This is important, for here is a book that is likely to be privately published. You may not have a contract, which normally gives some protection from trouble. Publishers don't want trouble any more than you do and won't print what you aren't sure about.

15. HOW-TO AND HOW-NOT-TO

Often local histories are printed by the local newspaper, which, while being expensive to start with, will give plenty of free publicity as they too would like to see your work sell, so that they can reprint it. If this happens, you will be in control of the design, jacket, illustrations and probably an index. Some writers make a real success out of producing their own books in this way. You need to be bit of an entrepreneur: confident, capable, with loads of business sense and used to getting your own way. Otherwise you may end up with something quite unlike what you had in mind. If you have those qualities though, you will probably enjoy promoting your book and it may do very well.

You can approach the bookshop where you normally shop for a signing, if you feel confident enough, while the Heritage or Historical Society may give a hotel launch, or failing this, a launch in the nearest library. You can build up a good relationship with the library and they will be helpful about stocking your book.

As with any kind of book, you need to consider your readers and what they want to find out. Let it be known that you are writing about this place and you won't be short of people to inform you. As you must be accurate, it's extra important to produce something that is a pleasure to read, well researched, stylish and neatly put together.

Local history – or local anything – are genres wherein you can consider self-publishing. It's a competitive trade, so prices have come down (slightly) and quality has gone up (a lot). Expect to pay most of the cost of production and to receive up to 40 per cent 'royalty' when the costs are cleared. Most subsidy or print-on-demand publishers are listed on the internet – be suspicious if they aren't – and you can find blogs from people who have employed them. These can be more revealing than anything they themselves might have to say. I think self-publishers are conscious of being the last resort, when all else has failed, but this is changing. For any type of book that is unlikely to sell more than 500 or 600 copies, try them out.

Vanity publishing and self-publishing

Vanity publishing has had such a bad press over the last decade or so that the remaining firms are keeping extremely quiet. You can still see a few advertisements from businesses that promise riches and fame in exchange for rather a lot of money. One victim told me that his 'free' copies cost him over £150 apiece.

There is some confusion regarding the words 'publishing' and 'printing'. Printing is just that. A printer expects you to pay him for printing your book. A publisher will not only pay you, but will, in addition to printing your work, get it edited, designed, promoted and distributed.

Between vanity and conventional publishing, a whole range of printers/publishers has sprung up in recent years. These include 'print-on-demand' publishers, who do just that, and online publishers, who may well kick-start a slightly risky book because they needn't print many besides the author's

15. HOW-TO AND HOW-NOT-TO

copies. Then if the online material is well received, the company may sell it to a conventional publisher.

'Print-on-demand' has become possible with the advent of digital printing. Once the initial run of books has appeared, you can get small numbers of copies at a fixed rate. Others give the writer a percentage, sometimes calling it a royalty. I have worked with some of these publishers for clients and only encountered one dodgy firm.

Self-publishing has to a great extent 'turned respectable'. There is plenty of choice of packages on the internet for you to check out. There is even *The Self-Publishing Magazine*, printed in the UK. It shows how things have changed. Such a title would have been laughed at a few years back. 'Writing magazines' carry plenty of advertisements for unconventional publishers of all kinds (the others don't need to advertise).

Back to the question, 'Will my self-published book pay me?' Probably not, is the answer, but the main reason is usually bad presentation, bad editing or a lack of know-how in the writer. If your book has been turned down by a dozen publishers without an encouraging word, the chances are that it won't make money for anybody. More than half of all self-published books are fiction. At present, publishers are fussier than ever about accepting novels. They need a great deal of marketing and promotion, which spells expense.

When a novel 'takes off', it really pays and a first-time author may find that he or she is somehow committed to writing a whole series of books. Catherine Cookson is a good example. Her books might not equal the latest 'chick-lit' offering in sales, but over the years, hundreds of thousands of her books have been sold. The copies in the libraries are dog-eared and have waiting lists. Crime writers have their devotees too, waiting for the next in the series to appear. There's an element of luck too. If *The Da Vinci Code* had been self-published, would it have been a runaway success? Perhaps.

There are thousands – no millions – of books out there on the Internet, to be read or downloaded. While technology advances all the time, so far they aren't as popular as was expected.

Vicious fights take place about copyright on the Internet, so get advice from someone familiar with the process. I have edited three books that first appeared online – two of them 'turned respectable', so to speak and were in the bookshops afterwards …

A vanity publisher may not even bind more than the 'free' copies and some review copies for the look of the thing. Their books are never reviewed.

Self-publishing has advantages for the specialist writer. In addition to the control you have over a commercial printer, you can get your book into print a great deal faster than a publisher can or will. This is because of the publishers' marketing schedules and half a dozen processes that the book must go through.

Then, you get all the proceeds once the initial payment is absorbed. Publishers pay only a small percentage and, if you have an agent, they will need their percentage as well. The way to work out which is best for you (provided that you

15. HOW-TO AND HOW-NOT-TO

can choose) is to reckon up how many copies you might sell at full price, less 35 per cent to a retailer, then get an idea of how many a publisher would expect to sell. Working with a publisher, the difference could run into thousands to your advantage and you would also get the recognition that do-it-yourself seldom provides. If you decide you'd be better self-publishing, do get a writer or editor that you trust to give an honest opinion first.

Then you might, like me, have a book, or booklet, printed locally and go on to have a longer version commissioned by a respected publisher.

Small houses, or presses, have been swallowed up by the big firms over the years, but there are quite a few left in Ireland. They include specialist and university presses and give the services of a big publisher, but with less reward for the writer. Again, if they land a winner, they are likely to try to pass the reprint rights on to a house with more clout.

It's easier to choose a specialist firm if you write, say, poetry, or books on religion or agriculture. Against the smaller rewards you might get – don't expect an advance – the atmosphere will be more personal and friendly.

Again, don't try to self-publish fiction. Not if you want to make money out of the venture.

Copyright

This is the property of the writer, even for a personal letter, but the recipient of the letter may sell it or publish it in their memoirs. Something to ponder for passionate letter writers.

Copyright is signed over to the publisher by contract, either for a fixed time or, more often, until the book is out of print and the publisher unwilling or unable to reprint. The copyright then returns to the author and then to his or her next of kin for seventy years after the author's death.

There is no copyright on titles. Call your book *War and Peace* if you must, or *PS I Love You* (there have been two books with that title in recent years). The law won't stop you, but your publisher will instruct you to think of something else.

There is no copyright on fact, but you are skating on thin ice here as there may be mixed opinions about what is fact. You can report facts already offered in print by someone else, but not in the same words.

When you enter a story or a play competition, read the small print. Sometimes, the writer has to hand over the publishing and/or performing rights for a fixed time. This could be a disaster for you.

Libel

I've mentioned libel briefly in the fiction section. Be careful, because a publisher's contract will protect the publisher rather than the author. The publisher will or should notice if there's anything potentially libellous in your book and will question you about it. If you have an agent, they will have already done this as part of their job.

15. HOW-TO AND HOW-NOT-TO

When going it alone, if in doubt ask a lawyer or get help from the Writers' Union or whatever organization you deal with.

A point to remember is that rape and insanity are not crimes, they are misfortunes, but to suggest either about a living person is defamatory. You can't libel the dead, but you can stir up a hornet's nest quite easily. Don't risk it.

One of the beauties of being a part-time writer is that you aren't going to be pressured into tackling a book that you feel is beyond your powers. 'I haven't time,' is a valid excuse. It's true; you haven't. 'Profit and pleasure' is a clichéd tag, but for you it can be a fact. Go for it!